50 DAYS, 500 MILES, AND 5 STATES WHEN I TURNED 50

Kelly Beane

For my mom:

Thank you for giving me the love of laughter, and for teaching me that being able to laugh at yourself is best of all. I miss your laugh every day.

CONTENTS

THE BING MOMENT

"You need a lot of looking after, don't you?"

I laughed at the older gentleman's evaluation of me; how could I not? He already had to show me how to operate the assortment of extra pop up trays and help me clean up my spilled cocktail after I chose the worst tray to place it on. Flying in first class was all new to me, and I was admittedly acting like a giddy schoolgirl. (Especially after finding out the drinks were free.) But a deep part of me recoiled at his words, being it's an assessment I've been fighting my entire life.

One doesn't really get the chance to learn about self-reliance when they marry at 18. I know you're expecting a tragic tale, but I have no regrets. I fell in love, and being deeply religious and devoted to following a certain path, when given the choice between early marriage and years of waiting for sex, I decided my honeymoon night could not come fast enough. Looking back, there are so many conflicting emotions about those restrictions and expectations that defined my holiness and worth. Though on the whole, I feel gratitude, even if I see things differently now.

How do I even begin to explain what happened when I entered my 40's? It's impossible to fully express in words the upheaval of everything that had given me security and a place of belonging. My identity as a "good Christian woman" had been cracked open like a nut, and I was terrified that what was inside could not survive. Ironically, Christianity teaches that life comes out of death, and I've found it to be true. My religious dead nut sprouted into a new way of seeing and being, but that's another story. This story is about how this new person I was becoming, for whatever reason, was calling me into the woods.

Not until I was 42 and only beginning my paradigm shift did I find her. No, I did not leave my husband for a woman if that's where you think this is going, though falling in love with the LGBTQ community is a large part of my growth that I will not go into here. Grandma Gatewood was who I found - just a short article about her that is. But she sparked the fire that would become my passion for backpacking. The oldest woman to complete the Appalachian Trail, and the first one to do it three times, I became mesmerized by the picture of the 67 year-old with Keds sneakers and boobs down to her bellybutton. As I gazed at the 1955 black and white photo of her, standing on the trail with a plain old over the shoulder sling bag, it seemed to me that nothing could be better than being a crazy old lady braving the wild.

It's pretty hard to live in Washington State and not have some kind of exposure to hiking. I, of course, had taken my kids on local trails for a day hike, and we all loved being outdoors and appreciating the beauty of undoubtedly one of the most scenic places in the world. Though, before I came across Grandma Gatewood's story, I had not backpacked a day in my life. I didn't even own one piece of gear - not even a daypack! My knowledge of long distance hiking was only a vague awareness of the presence of the Pacific Crest Trail running through the state and up into Canada. I wanted to know more about it, and with the help of the internet, a new world opened up to me.

I discovered that not only did the Pacific Crest Trail run 2,650 miles through our country, but there are also two other major long distance hikes in the USA: The 3,100 mile Continental Divide, and the East Coast's 2,184 mile Appalachian Trail. The more I read, the more entranced I became.

Hiker Lingo Term #1 Thru Hike: To hike an estab-

lished long distance trail from end to end.

Oh, to become an actual thru hiker! They had become like gods in my mind. No, my sensible self could not conceive of such a thing...but then there was this Grandma Gatewood. If she could do the Appalachian Trail (which let's face it, is on the East Coast where they don't even have real mountains) then that trail couldn't be all that hard, right? Still, there was no way I could justify the five to seven months it would take away from my family. Maybe I could do just a few weeks?

Then "bing," the thought of 50 days when I turned 50 popped into my brain. My 50th birthday was a long way off, but I needed time to figure out this whole backpacking thing anyway. Yes, eight years might be considered by many to be overkill; but as I said, I needed to take a very pragmatic approach. Dreaming big was not natural to me. I've always been more of a realist...some may even say a pessimist. (How negative is that?) But isn't life more palpable when you don't expect too much? Thankfully, the person I was becoming was starting to think differently, though 50 days was still all my baby optimistic mind could muster.

First things first, I needed to figure out where I would start and end. I read that the thru hiker "gods" supposedly averaged 20 miles a day, (BS in my opinion now) so I figured cutting that in half was a reasonable expectation. Ten multiplied by 50 equals 500, and more research revealed that 500 miles would take me through five states if I started in New York - the most "practical" place to fly into. And then another bing...50 days, 500 Miles, 5 States, all when I turned 50. No longer just a fun idea; this seemed like destiny! It was a perfect plan. I somehow had to make it happen.

Hiker Lingo Term #2 AT: Abbreviation for the Appalachian Trail. (I'll be using this from now on, because I swear to God, EVERY time I type Appalachian, I need to use spell check.)

So after a few obsessive months of googling all things AT, I realized I hadn't even gone on an actual backpack yet. Already struggling with back issues, I really had to come to terms with the fact that carrying 30 pounds around all day could be a deal breaker. My practical side (probably about 90% of me, which I guess is not exactly a 'side') could not go buying equipment without knowing for sure my real level of commitment to this "perfect plan." Blessedly, my friend Melissa had equipment to spare, so we set off on a sunny September weekday to conquer the Chain Lakes Loop atop the illustrious Mount Baker.

Of course, I made sure to set a reasonable goal of only eight miles on this two day trip - I mean, no need to try and showboat on your first trial run. Even so, the sheer volume of mistakes made was shocking...and hilariously thrilling too. Clearly, neither of us knew what we were doing, but it didn't matter. The mutual feeling of uncertainty was a bond; and that, combined with the excitement of being on our own, felt almost magical. Not one leading the other, but both of us wanting the experience as equals. It was new to me.

Not to make it sound like I was dominated and controlled in my younger years, but I had acquiesced to my husband the responsibility of taking care of just about everything for as long as I could remember. I hadn't much known the feeling of fear that comes with having the weight of responsibility of success or failure squarely on my own shoulders. But the more I hiked, especially alone, the more I discovered that the fear and stress created by self sufficiency also creates a pride I hadn't known. I was hooked. And though I didn't want to fall into the trap of making hiking the new thing that defined me and gave me identity, I felt a sense of belonging in the great outdoors that surprised me. Directionally challenged, forgetful, unorganized and unsure - basically a girl who needed a lot of looking after - and yet, the woods embraced me. Maybe only to eventually devour me, but it didn't matter. I was in love regardless.

GETTING TO SQUARE ONE

I'm going to state the obvious - this is not a story to impress. Doing one-fourth of the AT does not give you very big bragging rights; it's really not even worthy of an honorable mention. Last I looked, 290 people have not only completed the AT, but also the Pacific Crest (PCT) and the Continental Divide (CDT). That is a total of over 7000 miles, which is known in the hiking world as the "Triple Crown." And as if that isn't impressive enough, a handful of those triple crown achievers did so within one calendar year. Let me remind you, my mileage would be approximately 10 every day for a total of 50 days. Simple math will reveal that these few monster hikers had to average 27 miles every single day for an entire year - and for every day they missed hiking (which would be at least necessary in order to fly from one trail to the other) they did over 50. Miles. In one day. My mind can not even grasp it. So yeah, when people are doing that kind of shit, it's pretty difficult to be noteworthy.

And that's alright because my hike was much more about settling into a comfortable relationship with humiliation than glorying in people's praise. There would be no delusions of grandeur for me; I knew I'd be coming onto the trail with folks who had already been on it for at least a few months. I knew they would be blowing by me and doing far more miles than me. I didn't have anything to prove, I just wanted to accomplish what I considered a very doable goal. I set my bar low because

I wanted to give myself a fighting chance; I even hoped to relax a little some days and enjoy myself. But tripping over your low bar can be a tough pill to swallow, as it was clear I was in the weeds and way off the mark from the get go.

Relaxation? Not so much. Swallowing the "you may not even finish this" pill was the toughest, but I managed to get it down with a heavy dose of "just take one day at a time and see what happens." But let me first take you to the starting line.

As I already mentioned, practicality was my only reason for picking New York as my square one. I could get my plane ticket for free with my air miles, and I had read that there was a train in New York that took you directly to the trail. I wouldn't have to worry about buses or taxis; I only had to get myself to Grand Central Station. But somehow with all my calculations, I had failed to notice that 500 miles from the Appalachian Trail Railroad Stop would include six states instead of five. When I finally recognized this, I knew I had to scratch the railroad idea.

My new agenda would have to include more miles in New York so I finished before getting to Maine, or I had to forego hiking in New York altogether so Maine could be my 5th state. Obviously, there was no way I was going to ruin my homogenous grouping of numbers including five. Though whichever new start I chose, I knew I couldn't count on an easy train ride to the trail. I had to figure out another way to get myself to the AT.

The thought of maneuvering through the Big Apple alone was far more terrifying than the woods could ever be. As luck, or karma, or grace would have it, I discovered a past exchange student of ours was living and working in New York - only a half hour from the airport! Yumi had spent a whole school year with us and had become like family. And yes, she agreed to pick me up and get me to wherever I needed to go. I just needed to figure out where that would be.

Actually, I'm amazed I was ever able to settle on where to start. It's easy to get lost in the researching process. It's a beautiful and terrible thing, the amount of information about the AT. Before you know it, you are hours into someone's blog and wondering what it was you were even looking to answer-...only now your only question is, "TICKS!! WTF?!" Trying hard to keep myself from being distracted by YouTube videos on tick removal, I diligently scanned maps, looking for a good place I could jump on. This search for the perfect access spot started to feel like "pick a road, any road," because the AT crosses roads constantly. Then I discovered Yumi did not even have a car, so the hunt became even more challenging. My frugal sensibilities could not tolerate a huge Uber bill, and besides, I had Yumi to help me navigate the public transportation system. There had to be a good road near the trail that we could reach by bus...if only I could keep my mind off ticks long enough to find it.

At last, I thought I had found the perfect place right at the New York/Connecticut border. The blog I was reading showed a picture of a lovely “Welcome to Connecticut” sign I imagined myself posed in front of to commemorate "the beginning." This would place my 500 mile "end" at exactly the top of a mountain in Maine, where a bench to sit and ponder the beauty was mentioned; but also, more importantly, a road so I could get out of there. Though, as much as I could envision the “I did it!” photo of my sitting silhouette, gazing off to the rolling hills in contemplation of my life changing journey...I could also envision no cell reception to call for a ride, tears at wondering how to get the hell off the mountain, and a desperate hitchhike resulting in a kidnapping and my dead body in a ditch. Plus, if I started at the Connecticut border, the trail actually crosses back into New York for a few miles, and then we have the sixth state dilemma again.

I decided to approach the problem from a different angle - where did I want to end? When discovering my husband, Ken, wanted to meet and hike my last few days with me, a hotel room became my new priority. Is there a bedroom right on the trail in New Hampshire? In fact, there actually is! Reading about the huts in the White Mountains reminded me of our time in the Dolomites (one of our favorite parts of a two week trip we took to Europe) and I knew it would be the perfect ending for my 500 miles. Though, the shared rooms with bunk beds might dampen any romantic intentions. Then I noticed the "Joe Dodge Lodge," also directly on the trail, right in the middle of the Whites. A lodge could only mean a cozy fire, cocktails, and private rooms. Done. Counting backward 500 miles I found my starting line. Three hours on subways and buses and a walk through the small town of Greenwood Lake would bring me to my journey's start. My plan to hike in New York, Connecticut, Massachusetts, Vermont, and New Hampshire was set.

My sweet former exchange student was a lifesaver. Time Square was a daunting place, so as much as I wanted to have faith in my abilities to look after myself, I knew it would have taken me hours to find the right bus without her. The previous day of her showing me the sights had given me an appreciation for the humidity I was going to be dealing with, but the bus ride was my reality check for what East Coast rain looks like. Blue skies, turn a corner, windshields on full blast like we have entered a car wash, turn a corner, blue skies again. Departing the bus we were lucky enough to be on the dry cycle, but that was it for our luck for the day.

I knew from my research that the Village Vista Trail we would be using was nothing but a quick access route for hikers to get off the AT and into Greenwood Lake for resupply, and my directions for finding it were wonky at best. That's really not a good excuse for heading off straight away in the entirely wrong direction, but that's what happens when you are directionally challenged. It's why my husband laughed when I told him about my plans to become a long distance hiker - because finding my way through the wilderness was really the last thing I should be doing. I often had to take my phone with me when leaving a hotel room in case I couldn't find my way back, and I'm not even talking about driving. This was back before smartphones;

I just needed to call and be reminded what floor/room/elevator/complex/hallway/direction I needed to go in. Not a confidence booster for navigation abilities. My eight years of preparation improved my skills somewhat, but thank God for the invention of Google Maps, whose help got us turned in the right direction.

Arriving finally at the far end of a baseball park where the obscure sign signaled where the trail was, I tried to distract Yumi from the giant warning about ticks posted upon it. She was going to hike the first few miles with me until we reached a place where she could catch a bus home, and I wanted her experience to be a good one. The overgrown bushy path where we were to venture in looked like a tick obstacle course ("see if you can get through this without getting Lyme disease") though thankfully we somehow managed. Soon we hit a dirt road which you would think would be a no brainer to follow. And it was until we got to the end of it with no indicator as to where to go next. Lost and confused twice without even actually being on the AT. That has got to be a record.

Poor Yumi, forging ahead through the woods and calling back to let me know she sees something that looks like a trail, but I knew better. Nothing to do but backtrack and hope to find where we went wrong; and sure enough, a sneaky blue blaze guiding us off the road was missed when we took a corner.

> *Hiker Lingo Term #3 Blaze: A colored mark, usually painted on a tree or rock, about four inches tall by two inches wide. These are used to help guide hikers on the trail.*

Blazes are specifically color coded, and in this area, white is the color of the main trail, while blue is the color for going off trail to a town, shelter, store or easier route to avoid exposed parts of the trail in bad weather. Sometimes there are two stripes to indicate a change of direction, and sometimes there are three to indicate something I never did quite figure out.

We had to stop several times on that single steep mile leading up to the AT. I had read this path was horrible, so I wasn't discouraged, even being drenched in sweat and barely moving. I had taken several cheater trails to quickly gain access to the Pacific Crest Trail in Washington, so I believed that once we got on the actual trail, the going would be much easier. This understanding proved true at first. We intersected with the AT, and it was indeed easy and straightforward, with a white blazed tree every 70 feet or so. Yumi even mentioned getting anxious if she didn't see a blaze every few minutes, which made me laugh because the trail couldn't be more obvious even without them. There was no way I was going to have to worry about getting lost from here on out. Well, apart from the fact we missed the blue blaze we were supposed to follow to get to the ice creamery off trail, and had to turn around yet again, I felt confident any route confusion was behind me.

I wanted to stay until Yumi was safely on her bus, but I just couldn't risk getting to my first shelter in the dark. Many hikers don't mind traveling in the night air; some even prefer it. Not me. My very first attempt at a solo backpack back in Washington was mistimed, resulting in a complete fiasco of failing to get to my designated camp spot before dark. That memory of not being able to put together the borrowed tent I had no idea how to put up with the faint light of my cheap Walmart flashlight stills gives me anxiety - especially as dusk approaches. That first night being alone in the dark, cowboy camping in a field with mice crawling over me, was also my first experience with what might have been a panic attack; and I was in no hurry to repeat it. Therefore, to make sure I would have plenty of daylight to make it to the Wildcat Shelter, I reluctantly said a tearful goodbye to my Japanese daughter. With a stomach full of banana split and butterflies, I was on my own.

A ROUGH START

It didn't take long for my easy breezy dreams to be dashed. A few miles after leaving Yumi, and the clear cut path started to change into something quite a bit more challenging. This is when it started to become clear that the AT and the PCT are two different animals. Having hiked about half of Washington's PCT in bits and pieces over the years, I had the expectation that the AT should have the same "rules" about elevation gain. No more than a thousand feet in a mile had to be the grade because that's all the pack animals can handle. Why, in all my reading about the AT, I never clued in that it is most definitely not a pack animal trail with any such rules, is hard to comprehend. But the lights came on pretty quickly that day.

Suddenly the blazes were guiding me up what I considered a ridiculously steep rock face. Though once at the top, I took a few moments to appreciate the somewhat decent view, while snapping a couple selfies of course. I was here! I was actually doing this! Look at me!

And just like that, I was lost. Looking around to continue, I couldn't find the trail. The blaze painted on the rocky perch beneath my feet looked to be pointing straight off the cliff. This was more than trail confusion...this was trail treachery! I climbed back down, looking for any clue, but found nothing but a blue blaze, which I didn't understand at the time could also be a "how to skip the upcoming hard part" director. Continuing to look around, I spotted a small area I could possibly fit my tent and contemplated calling it a day until a more experienced hiker came along to show me how to follow the arrow to nowhere. That thought was too humiliating and drove me back up the rock to figure it out.

Examining again the blaze that I thought was an arrow, I decided it had to instead be a 90 degree angle, indicating a sudden change in direction. What a relief to finally see a glimmer of white paint on a rock behind me - basically back down where I was before the rock climb.

“Weird...that really difficult scramble seemed kind of pointless,” I thought. Due to my relief and excitement to be back on track, I laughed it off; but so began my understanding that the AT leads you up every rock, no matter how steep and basically unnecessary, because of the "vista." This pattern of suffering for pretty much the same view of rolling hills would result in much frustration, cursing, and tears. But so it is on the AT.

I don't know if I was disappointed or relieved when I finally arrived at the Wildcat Shelter and found myself completely alone. My oldest daughter had asked me before I left what I feared most about my quest. She was sure to Google "ways people die hiking," and jokingly warned me I shouldn't underestimate the danger of beavers. Though the answer I gave her surprised us both. Instead of saying ticks (or more specifically what they could give me) I responded before thinking, "feeling like an outcast with the other hikers." What a dumb fear when you could be mauled by a bear. But I knew realistically it would be my most difficult challenge. I have a deep desire to connect with people, along with a terrible understanding of how difficult and awkward it can be. So I was glad I didn't even have to try that first night. However, my other big fear of being raped and murdered was rearing its ugly head.

Of course, I wouldn't have mentioned that fear to my daughter. She didn't need that on her mind, though we both understand it's a fear all women have, whether they are in the woods or not. Even though it was a little difficult for me to make it to this shelter, I knew there was a road not too far away, with a much easier route. A group of rowdy guys could get there without much difficulty, with an entire case of beer in tow. The empty bottles already scattered about confirmed it probably happened frequently.

I pushed the scenarios I could create in my mind away. For the past eight years I had been jotting down all of my hiking lessons learned, and my previous year's nine day backpack provided me with a very profound one.

Hiking lesson #55: "Be careful with your imaginations."

Though it is true that tragic events happen in life, playing them out in your head does not prepare you to face them like you convince yourself it does. It only robs you of peace and makes you suffer through a false reality. I had suffered greatly on that trip by convincing myself a group of men who had passed my camp were going to come back to harm me when the truth was nothing of the sort. They hadn't done anything to warrant my believing this; it was simply the plot my fear had created. It had been two years since that horrid night of laying in my tent with my graphic imaginations, and I promised myself I would not make the same mistake again. If rowdy guys showed up at the Wildcat Shelter, I would have no choice but to deal with it. Until then, there was no reason to think about the what-ifs. Though, you know I still set my tent up in the woods as far away from the shelter as I could just the same.

The thunderstorm that hit that night astonished me. It was just a run of the mill East Coast storm (one of many to come) except I had never experienced anything like it. My West Coast senses were dumbfounded. As I laid there trying to fall asleep (always a difficult accomplishment on your first night) my thoughts turned to Yumi. I sure hoped she made it home safe. Why not see if I could reach her? Seeing a surprising couple of bars on my phone, I went ahead and shot her a text: "Are you home safe?"

"I'm having another journey. Lol."

Turns out New York buses are not the most reliable means of transportation. When it never showed up, Yumi ended up getting a ride with some random "old guy" to the station, then had to wait hours for the train into the city. I felt so guilty for leaving her alone that I stayed awake texting until she finally made it home. If anything would have happened to her, I would have never forgiven myself. When I finally got the okay to turn off my phone, it was almost impossible to relax. It took a long time, but eventually, I fell asleep to the lullaby of thunderclaps and hammering rain.

One day down, 49 more to go. It was not a great thought to wake up to. Even worse was thinking about the 14 miles I had to do to stay on task and make it to the Fingerboard Shelter. I had read the warnings on the thru hiker's blogs to not worry about having a set plan - some days you'd feel like hiking more than others, so don't worry about it and stay flexible. Except I wasn't a thru hiker, worrying is like breathing to me, and I don't like being flexible. So, I had 50 days laid out in stone on a carefully embossed sheet of paper, detailing each step of my perfectly thought out plan. It's so comforting, isn't it, knowing exactly how things are going to go? My previous hiking experience tried to teach me that things rarely go as expected (hiking lesson #48: Always remember that even though you think you have a plan, you don't really have a plan) and yet, it was still in my nature to believe I could control life with a precise itinerary. I had done plenty of 14 mile days before. Making up for the short miles on my first day was necessary to the overall master plan.

Except my legs were wanting to cramp just trying to get out of my sleeping bag. Maybe I had greatly underestimated how the climate would affect my body? Only a few miles into the day would confirm not only this but also the fact I had underestimated just about everything about this trail. Utterly stunned at the crazy inclines (rock scrambles, really) and unthinkably slippery declines, I deemed the AT insane by noon. More lightning and downpours ended my day at less than half my mile goal. Declaring "screw it," I pitched my tent right next to the trail where, well, you shouldn't be pitching anything.

“This is not how you are supposed to do this," I sulked, but mostly I was just thankful to be out of the rain. Eventually, I heard footsteps outside my tent, which was no surprise considering it was only midday.

"Rattlesnake here," a voice announced.

"Rattlesnake?!?! WHERE?"

"No...I mean my trail name is Rattlesnake. You sure have a crappy spot here," he replied.

Double idiot strike. Newbie loser status confirmed. I used the excuse that going any higher didn't seem wise with all the lightning, but he was having none of it. The threat of death is usually not much of a deterrent to the thru hikers, so away went the footsteps. I was still too excited being out there to be overly discouraged, though packing up in the morning amid the still persistent rain was diminishing my enthusiasm considerably. Just as I was finishing up, a section hiker coming south introduced himself as "Snickers" while he handed me several snack size ones. Even though he only had about 100 miles in Connecticut to complete the whole trail, he explained that he was redoing this section because it was his favorite. Standing there soaking wet and sporting a cheesy grin, he made an up and down roller coaster motion with his hand (as in "weee, isn't this fun?") then handed me a couple more candies and exclaimed with far too much earnestness to "have a great day." As much as I wanted to be annoyed and counter with, "I'd prefer a merry-go-round right about now,” I couldn't help being a little cheered by his optimism...plus the chocolate didn't hurt either.

I have a confession to make. Only a couple hours into my day I ended up dumping half my white gas out. This was after lowering my pack down another crazy steep decline because my legs felt like jello. I couldn't believe how heavy my pack had become. Having everything wet did, of course, make it heavier, but I swear it felt like a dead body. (Yes, I was using a backpack cover. With that kind of rain, staying dry is pretty impossible no matter what gear you are using.) And so, I dumped the gas right there on the forest floor like some kind of environmental terrorist. I'm sorry. I plead insanity. I couldn't think of anything else to lighten the load, and I was desperate. When Katz from "A Walk in the Woods" unloads half his pack right on the trail in a fit of exhaustion, everyone laughs, so I'm hoping I can be forgiven as well.

Soon after that transgression, I met "Citizen," who asked if I wanted to hitch a ride with him to town because he needed, of all things, gas. As if looking to be absolved, I blurted out my crime to nature. I felt even worse about my sin now that I knew I could have avoided it and helped him out at the same time. Though he, like almost every other hiker I met out there, was using the canister type gas instead of white gas like me. Ironically, I choose my stove because I didn't like the idea of the wastefulness of the canisters, along with never knowing for sure how much gas was left inside them until you ran out. I felt a little better knowing he couldn't have used my squandered gas anyway, but let him know I was too behind in miles to go into town with him. Before his much faster pace left me in the dust, we hiked together for a few minutes while we approached the upcoming road. He asked me my trail name.

> *Hiker Lingo Term #4 Trail Name: A nickname used by a hiker during their hike. Generally given by other hikers, it should reflect your personality, appearance, style of hiking, or some quirky thing that you do on the trail.*

Even though it was only my third day, I was already tired of explaining I didn't have a trail name yet. I was well aware of the rule stating I couldn't name myself and explained as much to Citizen.

"I named myself," he said proudly. "I'm not trusting people I hardly know to give me some idiotic name I hate."

Thus having received permission, I christened myself as "Kellbell," the username for every hiking website I had been on for the past eight years. It felt right. Yes, I also felt a little like a cheater who was missing out on a right of passage I had waited all these years to obtain. But primarily I felt this was a moniker that had always been mine. It was who I was, and I didn't want to change it. Though had I known half the time I'd be called "Cowbell," I may have reconsidered.

When it finally stopped raining, the trail was the most flooded it would be for the next 47 days. Thankfully I had opted to bring my heavier but sturdier Tevas instead of my usual flip flops for camp shoes (which I purchased at a thrift store for only a few bucks...there's no way I could ever bring myself to spend more than $30 on sandals) so I switched into them. For the better part of the day, I was at least ankle deep in water. It was unbelievably slow going, but I was bound and determined to make it to the shelter I was supposed to have camped at the previous night. I kept referring to the page I had ripped out of the "Northbound A.T. Guide" book I had brought with me. Although lacking proper maps, I still believed this miraculous book with its mile-to-mile descriptions of every upcoming stream, shelter, or intersecting trail was all I needed for navigation. And for the most part, it was, though to an overthinker like me it may have offered a bit TOO much information.

I didn't need to know that the AT and the Red Dot Trail would be merging - I really only needed to keep focusing on the white blazes to keep me on track. But because the book made a note of it, my conclusion was that I'd be following the red dot markers for the portion of the trail where they were combined. I was a mile from Fingerboard when the white dots with a red round center started appearing on the trees and rocks, so I kept my eyes peeled and intently searched for them like I was on a demented Easter egg hunt - for almost an hour - at which time I thought I really should have gotten to the shelter already. Frustrated, exhausted and ready to be done, I dug out my sacred page of instruction once again to try and figure out what I was missing. With horror, I now noticed the tiny indicator of (.01) after the notation of the red dot merge. A tenth of a mile?!? I was only supposed to be following the red dots for a stinking tenth of a mile?! Fuck me. (Yes, this is where I started kicking up my cursing frequency. I think I reached sailor status by the end.)

So, where the hell was I? With panic mode descending quickly, I remembered I had downloaded an app that supposedly showed where I was at all times while on the AT. Though it seemed too good to be true, it was worth a try. As I expected, I couldn't make heads or tails of it. Why should I think I could? I can barely use email on my phone; what was I thinking downloading this stupid thing?

And then I took my only logical course of action...a complete hysterical crying breakdown fit. I'll just lay down here in a heap and wallow in self-deprecation. Why not? There is just so much to criticize in myself. I mean, this could take a while.

Except I knew I should be smart and backtrack - an hour is really not a terminal mistake, after all. But I just couldn't. Not only did I hate the thought of wasted miles, but I was also afraid I wouldn't be able to find my way back to the AT and become even more lost. This part of the trail was just one large rock; very expansive and difficult to navigate. I would even say impossible, except for the randomly scattered dots painted along the way, and they were not that easy to find. When my pity party concluded, I decided to keep going forward and embrace the adventure, wherever it led. As long as I could keep finding the red dots, they had to lead somewhere.

And they did! Ten minutes or less forward, and there was

the shelter. I didn't even care how it was possible, I was only grateful to have made it. There was even a cute couple already camped out there - my first night with company! Oh, bless the trail gods, I was euphoric. Yet as much as I wanted to baste in the bliss and comfort of all being well with the world, I had to admit to myself that something felt off.

"This is the Fingerboard shelter, right?" I asked the love-birds with as much confidence as I could muster.

The look they gave me confirmed all my fears. Of course, the AT is not the only trail with shelters, but sometimes we want something to be true so bad that we ditch logic. I'm glad I had no pride left at that point and spilled my guts to them about how lost I was. They had an excellent map with them, which they allowed me to take a picture of so I could attempt to steer myself through the 2.4 miles back to the AT the next day. Though extremely appreciative of the hope of salvation the picture provided, thinking about the spider vein maze of intersecting trails I had to face come morning light gave me another fitful night's sleep.

FIRE, GUNS, AND TATTOOS, OH MY

It took me two hours to make it to "Times Square." No, not the famous one in Manhattan, but the major five trail intersection the other hikers kept warning me about. When I got there, I sat down to rest and stared at the giant rock painted with the junction's nickname, and wished it also had arrows directing me to exactly which path was the correct one. The map picture I had on my phone should have been enough to give me assurance, but I am always one to second guess myself. Five different trails to choose from - somehow I would find a way to talk myself out of picking the right one, I just knew it. I finally made my choice and tried to feel confident, but after another hour with no shelter in sight, I lost all faith and fell down the dark hole of despair. Just as the hot tears were welling up, I heard voices ahead. Far too desperately, I practically ran to them, announcing I was lost and needed help.

"Don't you worry, Mam, we have lots of maps. We will get you pointed in the right direction," they comforted me. "Where're you trying to get to?"

"I'm just trying to get back on the AT," I answered with some embarrassment.

Ready and waiting for their looks of pity and "tisk, tisk, poor girl is way off track" glances at each other, I tried to set my mind on gratitude for being helped, instead of frustrated over the added miles. I would take my lumps with a "thank you" instead of sobs.

"You're not lost! Ten more minutes and you are there!"

With only three full days under my belt, I knew I had to stop putting myself through such emotional turmoil with all my self-doubt. Yes, I had gotten off trail and was behind schedule, but I am not incapable and on the verge of defeat at every turn. I had to find a way to stop convincing myself I was failing ...but how?

Thankfully the answer was just a few hours away.

I met Little Debbie and Gaucho when I was a little less than a mile from my goal. Now that my very carefully planned itinerary was annihilated, I was doing my best to improvise without throwing my tent up all willy nilly, as I had done on my second night. I was also determined to be as driven as possible, knowing I had a full day to make up. Therefore, I made the North Mountain Shelter the day's ambitious aim, and I was ready to be there already.

The hiking duo was loading up on water for their push up the upcoming dry mountain. Nobody likes hauling extra weight, so they were arguing about just how much water they actually needed.

"Do you have the Guthook's app?" they turned to me to ask.

"Yes, but I haven't a clue how to use it," I answered sheepishly. "I've already gotten lost and it didn't help at all." (Actually, I think I remember saying it was "fucking useless" - which is not my usual MO - though it became more so every day.)

"You purchased the maps, right?"

Purchase? Who said anything about purchasing anything? This app was supposed to be free, which is the only reason I downloaded it. But they went on to explain that you had to buy the maps if you wanted it to work, though you could opt to just get the section you were on instead of spending a lot on the entire trail. Once the map was downloaded, your "dot" would appear on the trail with amazing precision. They even joked about their friend using it for help after he wandered too far from the trail to poop.

"It also has a community forum where other hikers give advice or tell you where there is water that isn't mentioned in the AT Guide," they further explained. "We don't have the app, but we were hoping we could use yours to see if there's actually more water ahead so we don't have to carry so much."

Without cell service, I couldn't purchase what was needed to help them out, but I knew that even though I'm as cheap as hell, I would be giving Mr. Guthook my money ASAP. Once I could get those magic maps to work, I believed the problem of my constant state of anxiety would be answered. I would later discover that - as it is with so much in life - the thing we think will solve all of our problems can be the very thing which creates yet another problem. You will hear all about that soon enough.

After loading up with my own water, I started my way up. Less than a mile - I only had less than a mile. This is what I kept reminding myself, over and over, because the day felt like it would never end. Motivating myself with the dangling carrot of how good it was going to feel to actually make it to my goal for the day, I kept putting one foot in front of the other. And once again, after over an hour, still no shelter.

I tried to get my feet to move a little further with the promise that it had to be just around the corner, but I was done. I was too tired to hope it was just ahead. Too tired to berate myself for failing. Too tired to worry if I was somehow off trail again. Too tired to be mad about the fact my stuff was all wet because the extra water I had loaded up on had leaked. Too tired to be concerned about camping illegally. I was too damn tired to care about anything, period.

Anything except for food, that is.

Once my tent was situated all kitty wampus on the flattest

little shred of somewhat un-bushy ground I could find, I set up my trusty Whisper Light stove to cook my meal.

Going about my routine of pumping the gas, adjusting the pressure, lighting the flame, then waiting for the exact moment you need to adjust the pressure again so it doesn't go out, I had to question why I felt the need to choose a "real" stove instead of the less complicated JetBoil. I guess I figured, why take the easy route when I can make my life as difficult as possible? If I had known my need to prove myself would result in such a catastrophe, I most definitely would have figured differently.

I couldn't tell you exactly what I did wrong, except that I did it wrong in a big way. So much flame - and things were on fire that shouldn't have been. The following minutes were the most terrifying of the whole trip...possibly my whole life.

"Washington Hiker Burns Down New York" - I could see the headlines already.

If I made it out alive, I would stay in these mountains forever. Living out the rest of my days in hiding would probably be my best bet. The only thing I remember doing was repeating "Help me, Jesus," over and over. And blessed be, my desperate plea was heard. Somehow, without any help from a functioning brain, I managed to not catch everything on fire. In addition to giving plenty of thanks, I decided that if I ever pushed myself that hard again, I would just settle for a granola bar.

I kept expecting to come across the West Mountain Shelter the following day but I never did. Besides being very grateful I hadn't kept pushing the previous night, I was completely baffled. I knew I was still on the AT (thanks to the white blazes) so I couldn't understand how I had missed it. Finally, some other hikers informed me I would have had to hike a half mile off-trail to reach it; making me incredibly glad that even if there had been a sign or blue blaze to the North Mountain Shelter, I had somehow overlooked it.

I was also very glad to have other hikers around to set me

straight on that kind of stuff. That last big trip I mentioned taking before coming to the East Coast gave me more than just lesson #55. One of the most important things I learned on that nine day lonely trek was how much better life is when other people are around. Even though I fear others judging me as a strange oddball, having no one at all to worry about judging me is even worse.

For several of those nine days on that final preparation hike, I didn't see a soul. It was awful. Even though I really enjoy solo hiking, that trip made me realize how much I need small encounters with others. A quick stop on the trail and a few minutes of conversation are all that are required to be comforted with the feeling of being a part of a community. Being around other hikers gives you the sense that though you might be alone, you're not really alone.

Hiking down from Bear Mountain that day I was really hoping to run into more hikers because I needed a different kind of reassurance. I needed someone to tell me I wasn't crazy for hearing gunfire. The sound I was hearing was not just normal gunfire, as in a possible shooting range nearby, but huge sustained bursts from what sounded like a machine gun.

I allowed my mind to wander to visions of an active shooter in the middle of the road I was heading towards, blasting everything in sight. So much for controlling my imaginations. What a ridiculous thing to think about...but what if it wasn't? Either way, I did know I wasn't too keen on getting down the hill in any big hurry. Finally, some day-hikers were coming towards me.

"Hey there! Do you happen to know if that's gunfire I'm hearing?" I tried to ask in a casual fashion.

"Oh yeah. West Point is not far away. They must be doing drills."

Duh. Why did I not think of that? Maybe because my brain just loves to jump to the worst-case scenario. Why I felt the need to then tell them my paranoid anticipation of upcoming carnage still confounds me. Perhaps I believed a confession of my neurotic fantasies would come across as charming? Instead, they just looked at me like I was an idiot. Damn it, it sucks not having your oddball-ness appreciated.

As soon as I was down that mountain, I had to go straight up another, which is, unfortunately, par for this course. These were some of the driest mountains around, and as most of the water I had hauled up the night before had leaked out due to failing to tighten my water bag good enough, I was in a desperate situation. My hiking bible promised vending machines at the lookout tower coming up, so the hope of a cold Snapple was the only thing keeping my legs working. I don't know about you, but when my need is at the 100% level like it was that day, I tend to obsess.

"What if the machines aren't there? What if they only have candy bars? What if there is only one drink available and when I press for it, I see the word empty?"

Having arrived at last, I pictured a possible scene of me wildly kicking the machine like a lunatic if it didn't deliver. Did you know your odds of dying from a vending machine falling on you are almost the same as getting killed by a bear? It's true; so I cautiously made my way to the glowing appliances with a resolve to control any overwhelming feelings of disappointment.

Drinks galore! Including Lemonade Snapple (I know I'm copying Cheryl Strayed, but they really are the best) and chips to boot!! This is the agony and joy of hiking, and exactly why I love and hate it so much. When else would a cold sugary drink and a bag of Doritos bring you to grateful tears?

After enjoying my bounty, I headed down, down, down to the lowest elevation on the entire AT - the deceptively named Trailside Zoo. First of all, the trail does not go on the side of the zoo, but literally right through it. Secondly, it's about as much of a zoo as a pet store. What a sad little place. Though impressively, it did have bears. I had fun positioning a picture of them in such a way as to fake out my friends - tricking them into thinking I was having an actual wild encounter. Even so, I felt terrible for those poor animals in their dingy little home.

There were plenty of other hikers mulling around the zoo as I made my way through, but the older man waiting in the horrendous line at the concession stand is the one I remember most. As much as I craved any sort of real food, after 10 minutes of standing in the hot sun while hordes of teenagers were taking forever to decide what to order, I gave up and settled for an ice cream from the nearby vending machine.

Eating my treat in the shade and watching this elderly man wait so patiently, I was amazed he was not losing his shit. He had a tag on his pack signifying he was a thru-hiker - so he had already hiked 1403 miles, with 787 still to go. If those kids had understood this, I'm sure they would have let him cut. In fact, I should have gone over there and demanded it.

"Can you not smell this man?! Let me tell you, he's been through hell! I don't care that you can't settle on chicken fingers or nachos - move your fat asses over and let him get his damn burger already!!"

But alas, I didn't. And I'll never know if he endured that outrageous line long enough to get his well deserved fill.

I camped illegally again that night. Actually, I'm not sure if it was illegal. Unlike some of the other states, there are no warning signs indicating you were expected to stay only in the designated areas in New York. But I knew at best it was bad form. Unfortunately, my exhaustion was turning me into a bit of an asshole, because I didn't care. As I holed up in my tent right next to a stream, I heard other hikers passing by and hoped they didn't think too badly of me. Finally, the night came, and with it, the sounds.

Although being alone in the woods at night is never easy, it becomes easier. My first night ever, as I already mentioned with my first panic attack, was one of the worst of my life. But the next night was easier - and so on, and so on. Even though some nights are worse than others, (depending on the sounds you hear) the more times you do it, the more acclimated you become.

I was already becoming more at ease on this trip, but even so, this particular night I kept hearing things in my sleep that I couldn't process. Had I been fully awake, I think I would have realized there were hikers camped up the hill beyond me, but it took one of them coming down in the morning to get water before I put all the pieces together.

Expecting a lecture on why I shouldn't be camped there, I was hesitant to make conversation. But he actually complimented me on my spot and introduced himself as "For Now." He explained that he was a budding tattoo artist and giving them out for free to anyone interested. I found his trail name ironic for someone who was handing out something so permanent, and admitted I wasn't quite ready for such a forever gift.

"Maybe after you've been out here a little longer," he answered with a sly grin, and back up the hill he went.

"Man, I'm glad I'm not having to haul water up that hill just to make my breakfast," I thought as I watched him leave. Though later, as I passed their little camp, I felt a pang of regret. If I would have just gone a little further, I would have found the more established site (not mentioned in my AT Guide--some bible that turned out to be) and then maybe I would have experienced some of the connection and camaraderie I was hoping to be a part of.

But yet again, I also felt relief; fearing that being with others would have only proven true my worries of feeling like the odd man out (or in this case, old woman) completely true. It's the conflict of needing companionship but fearing rejection even more. Pretty much the human struggle in a nutshell, wouldn't you say?

ARE WE HUNGRY YET?

Day seven brought with it a case of the squirts. Right under the fear of humans and ticks would be biggest fear #3: Bodily function issues. Dehydrating my own crab meat might not have been the best idea. My husband had bought me a food dehydrator for Christmas, and my dad had dropped off a bunch of free crab right before I left, so I figured why not? I had become obsessed with saving money on food costs, and therefore made quite a few choices I lived to regret. If only I would have just brought with me the cash I spent shipping my crappy cheap food ahead, and instead trusted I would have plenty of opportunities to resupply along the trail, but hindsight is always 20/20.

Case and point, the previous day's hike had brought me directly to a convenience store. With all the exhaustive notes about upcoming footbridges, lookout towers, and dirt roads, for some reason my guidebook didn't think running into groceries was worth mentioning. Wandering into the establishment, I kind of froze. I knew I should probably buy stuff, considering I was two days behind and therefore running low on food, but I felt guilty about all the money I already spent shipping the supplies that I knew were waiting for me in a few days' time. Plus, I was suddenly acutely aware of my stench. So I grabbed just a couple of ridiculous items and bolted. Don't get me wrong, I was thankful for the banana and ding dong, but a clearer mind would have dropped a few more bills for something more substantial.

I had another opportunity the following day at Clarence Fahnestock State Park. I found the noted "concession stand" was actually more of a cafe, offering not only the holy grail of a burger and fries but also a fairly large array of items I could have loaded up on if I hadn't felt stressed about money. But at least I did splurge on the burger and fries.

I sat for a long time trying to finish everything because I knew I needed the calories. Shouldn't eating be the easiest part of this whole endeavor?

> *Hiker Lingo Term #5 Hiker Hunger: An insatiable, bottomless hunger that torments thru-hikers and allows them the ability to scarf everything in sight when given the opportunity.*

I had read about "hiker hunger," and was wondering when it might overtake me. I'll tell you right now, it never did. I loved the idea of food, including the first few bites, but then it became increasingly difficult to continue. And you know if this was true for fries, it was especially true of the shitty food I made at camp. There would be nights I'd divide my little meal into bite-size sections, and then like some draconian parent creating food issues, force myself to eat each one every five minutes until I was done. Hard to believe, but it was one of the hardest parts of the trip. I am not one who normally struggles with eating, so I found this phenomenon most unnerving. I later heard from other hikers that it is not completely uncommon; though that didn't make it any less troubling.

Trying to force down every last fry, I noticed another hiker at a table not far from me. My anti-social self wanted to ignore him, but the better part of me saw my unfinished food as an opportunity to make conversation. And it worked! He told me about how he had come from Germany, how he got gotten his trail name - all the nice small talk. Finally, an interaction that lasted more than a couple minutes; maybe I can pull off extrovert after all! Plus, he gladly ate all my fries.

Being that I was having such bad luck making it to the shelters, I tried not to get my hopes up that I'd reach what my guide referred to as "RPH." (Ralph's Peak Hikers' Cabin) Reading the notes about which franchises would deliver pizza there, I was confused and intrigued by what to expect. That it was obviously accessible by road, and the fact I was a single woman hiker, made me apprehensive. Single woman hiker plus creepy pizza delivery man equals a Dateline episode I didn't want to be starring in. I was so relieved to arrive to a group of hikers who were already there. Except now I knew there was no place to hide, and I had to face my biggest fear. Time to step up my social game.

I figured my inability to finish a whole pizza would work to my advantage in this scenario. If sharing my fries worked earlier, giving away pizza was going to win me all kinds of love. Would you believe almost half of these people were vegan or vegetarian? That should be against hiking law. So now I feared getting stuck with half a pizza in a "cabin" that was missing a wall, where heaven help us, any bear could wander in for a midnight snack.

"Conversation" I was hoping to strike up became me mostly just asking the others if they were sure they didn't want another slice. The uncomfortable air of feeling like nobody was much in the mood to talk, combined with my already paranoid assumptions that I didn't fit in, was proving my worst fear a legitimate one.

Thank God for "Lightning Rod." Besides eating most of the pizza, he recognized me from earlier that day when he blew by me so fast and stealthy that he nearly caused me a heart attack - not just once, but twice. We laughed, and it broke the air. Before long a group of us were sitting outside comfortably telling stories. Well, mostly they told them, but I was just grateful to be blending in.

I did have my one anecdote about the red dot blunder, but like most thru-hikers, Lightning Rod had an even better one. I believe it was 12 miles he deviated, onto someone's private property. When the owners came across him, instead of kicking him off, they brought him into their home, fed him, then drove him back to the trail. Way to be a one-upper, LR...but it was a great story.

When darkness descended, the lightning bugs came out. What an entirely magical moment. Part of me didn't want the night to end, but I was spent; even more so mentally than physically. Stepping up my social game was far more exhausting than hiking.

Even though half the group had their tents set up in the surrounding yard, I determined this was the best opportunity I would have to actually sleep in a shelter. This was part of the whole AT culture I knew I wanted to experience. I got myself all situated on a bottom bunk and tried to fall asleep. OMG, how is it possible for it to be this hot? Open sleeping bag, one arm and leg out...that's a little better. Then, OMG, how are there so many mosquitoes in here? Slap, slap, slap...arm and leg in again. Rinse and repeat.

In addition to my extreme discomfort was the self-conscious awareness that I was surrounded by others who were also trying to sleep and could hear my every move. Suddenly my air mattress was the loudest object on the entire earth. And God forbid if I should have to fart. But again, this is part of what it means to do this hike. Suck it up, it's one night for heaven's sake.

I don't think it was another hour before I gave up. "Naked and Afraid" contestants, you have my full admiration for enduring insects night after night. I just couldn't. So as quietly as I could, which was not quiet at all, I got my tent and headlamp and went outside. I managed to get the tent up without my light because folks were out there too, and I was trying my best not to annoy absolutely everyone. Finally, I had a force field against the demon bugs, and now that I had privacy I could undress and cool down. Once my sports bra was off, I touched something on my breastbone that felt suspiciously like slugs. Having previously found one in my shoe, it did not seem as unlikely as you might otherwise think.

Though of course, it did seem wrong in every way imaginable. Somehow managing not to scream, I peeled them off and threw them down post-haste. Great, now I have slugs in my tent. I really, really, really did not want to even see them; but having them sliming around free would not allow for very restful slumber. Getting my headlamp on, I looked down with great foreboding, only to find my earplugs. Confused at first, I suddenly remembered I had shoved them down my bra so as not to lose them, where apparently they had adhered in the sticky heat. It was all I could do to keep from laughing out loud and waking everyone up.

Moments later it started to rain. Because I was in such a hurry and trying to keep quiet, I hadn't brought my rain fly with me. Damn it, I'm going to have to go back in the cabin. I decided if I was going to be that big of a pain in the ass, I might as well go all in. I picked up my tent, shoved it through the door loud as hell, and slept right there in the middle of the floor. Sleeping in your tent inside a shelter probably didn't count for the full AT experience, but it was the best I could do.

I apologized profusely in the morning for the night's nonsense, though "Traveler" only thanked me for waking him so he could rescue his hanging clothes from the rain. It was sad leaving when I was just starting to feel a bit of kinship, and I hated knowing with my much slower pace, I'd most likely never see any of them again. Thankfully I was wrong, as Lightning Rod would strike many more times before my hike was over.

PHONES AND MEN...CAN'T LIVE WITH THEM, CAN'T LIVE WITHOUT THEM

My addiction started just after the end of the first week. Phone use was something my previous hiking experience did not allow for much of. My beloved Washington's PCT has very limited cell coverage, which for me is part of its appeal. Getting yourself off-grid is kind of the main point of going into the woods, isn't it? But the AT is a different animal in so many ways.

It was strange to be able to look at my phone at almost anytime and see what was going on in the real world. At first, I didn't like it, because it felt counterproductive to the experience I was wanting to have. But I had never been away from family and friends for much longer than a week, so it makes sense that my resolve to not continually check my phone would crumble around this time.

I was so needy for the feeling of connection, I started to use my phone as a motivator... "You can look at a Snapchat when you get to the top," and so forth. But in addition to trying to keep my social media fix to a minimum, I was really trying to keep from becoming totally reliant on my Guthook's app.

Hiker Lingo Term #6 False Peak: A peak that appears

> *to be the pinnacle of the mountain, but upon reaching it, it turns out the summit is higher. Sometimes this term is used to refer to anytime you think you've reached your goal, but haven't.*

The false peak fake-out is always the hardest part of hiking for me. This syndrome happens all the time. You are SURE you are almost there, ("It has to be just over that hill/only another 10 minutes MAX/I think I see it just ahead") only to discover you have completely fooled yourself and still have a long way to go. Having the ability to know exactly where you are at all times puts an end to this agonizing self-deception. Being able to keep myself in check was the best thing the Guthook's app could have ever done for me. Though there were days when this ability became its own torment.

"You just checked...it said a mile to go, remember? You don't need to check again. Just keep going, you'll get there eventually," I would remind myself.

"But it feels like I should have gotten there by now. A mile is not far. Why is it not here? Maybe I missed it. Just check, you'll feel better," I argued with myself.

"You are being such a pain in the ass. It's not going to make you feel better. Do you think you've gone a mile? How are you going to feel when you find out you've only gone half a mile? Not better, I can tell you that. And besides, you are going to use up all your phone charge if you keep looking, and then you won't have it when you really need it. Stop thinking about it and just hike," I would scold myself.

"I know you are right...but if I look and it says I only have a tenth of a mile left, it will help. I'll be encouraged and stop obsessing," I would appeal to myself.

Then I would finally give in, only to find that I had over a half mile to go. I cannot tell you how often this happened. The last mile is always the worst. Sometimes I'd check up to five times in that last mile, I'm not even kidding. It's embarrassing to admit.

Getting to Morgan Stewart Shelter was one of those days. After arguing with myself for over an hour, I was an emotional mess by the time I finally got there. As usual, I felt the same relief/disappointment conflict about being there alone. (Not counting the one tent I could see pitched in the trees.) I actually felt more disappointment than relief that the tent folk didn't come out to say hi, probably due to the previous night's social successes. Yes, it was difficult getting through the awkward air at RHP, but overall I really did enjoy being around others. So now that I was sitting and eating my meal by myself, a sudden feeling of loneliness hit hard.

This shelter provided a picnic table, so at least I had a nice spot to cook, though I didn't get the chance to actually dine there. I had to grab my stuff and retreat full throttle to my own tent, due to the mosquitoes suddenly descending like a fog. I felt bad that I had judged whoever was out back as anti-social for not coming out to greet me, (hypocrisy is the easiest of sins) because obviously, they stayed in their tent knowing that mosquito hour would soon be upon us.

Several more hikers came in after that, but the mosquitoes were going nowhere, so we all stayed put in our demon bug force fields. The morning was not as bad, so some of us ventured out to the table for breakfast, at which time one of the girls seemed put off that I asked her name.

"We already met. Don't you remember me? I'm Debbie."

I didn't remember. Embarrassed, I said I had met a lot of people and had a bad memory. I could tell she thought it was a lame excuse, which it was, and every time I ran into her after that she gave me the cold shoulder. I never got the chance to explain that had she used her full trail name, "Little Debbie," it would have clicked...I mean shit, that's what the trail names are for.

Little Debbie was part of what I would later call the "party crew." Though at least twice my speed, I would continue to leapfrog with them because they spent so much time hanging out smoking pot. Lightning Rod became my favorite crew member, as we would always have a little banter when we passed each other; but I dreaded seeing Little Debbie. Maybe I was just paranoid, but I was sure she didn't like me.

Halfway through this day, I passed some of the crew swimming in a perfect lake. I joked that I would love to swim too, except I didn't want to wash off my now half inch coating of deet; which though exaggerated, was true. More true was that I would never feel comfortable crashing their party, and even if I did, I didn't have the time. Today was the day I needed to pick up my food, and the place I had shipped it to closed at 5:00 pm sharp. I barely had time to stop and eat, much less lake frolic.

Sometimes it was a little hard not to be jealous of the party crew. It seemed a cruel injustice to plod forward hour by hour, day after day, while these punks made up all my arduous miles in mere hours after lounging around in their weed induced haze. But then I would remember being young, and consequently decide I'm fine with being old and slow. I had my time, and I can't say I miss it much. Besides, we all know the turtle wins in the end.

Guthook's let me know I'd better kick it into high gear if I wanted to get to my food in time. Native Landscaping was where I was headed; a hiker friendly business that would hold supply shipments at no cost and was only slightly off-trail. In the opposite direction, and a little further off-trail was Tony's Deli, where I planned to stay the night. Knowing I would have to pass Native Landscaping again the following morning, in order to get back on the trail, I decided my food could wait until then. Keeping it in low gear was all I had left.

I was looking forward to a good meal at the deli. The notes in my book said camping in their yard was allowed, which seemed strange, but I didn't see another option. I'm not a big fan of hiking on a busy highway, but a half mile was necessary in order to get there, so I tried to kick it into at least second gear. When I saw Tony's Deli just ahead, a car coming towards me pulled over and stopped right in front of me. As I walked by the car, a man rolled his window down and offered me water. What. The. Hell. Maybe he was just being nice, but if that was the case, he was clueless about the lives of women. How could he not know that a solo female hiker would be freaked out by this supposed kind gesture? It wasn't like I was miles away from water on some desert road and needed help. It felt very sketchy, so I only shook my head and quickly passed by him. But the episode planted an uneasiness in my gut.

What can I say about Tony's Deli? Good prices, decent food, accommodating staff...and whack. With a floor so sloping you feel you are walking on the deck of a ship, and a scary little bathroom out the back door with a sign saying you can't wash your dishes, it was very whack. And I haven't even gotten to the "camping area." A grassy strip to the side of the building with a few random deteriorating plastic chairs and a Little Tikes playhouse that looked like it had been there since the '80s, it was double whack. But that was okay, because here I was, wearing the same clothes for over a week and brushing my teeth every other day. I could hang with whack.

Setting up my tent, I kept considering the highway that was right there. The uneasy feeling the guy in the car left in my gut kept growing. What was keeping any weirdo from pulling over and assaulting me? I tried to stop the scary thoughts by assuring myself hikers stayed here all the time, though the fact nobody else was there was not helping. I went back inside to get a bite to eat and distract myself from my fears.

The folks working there were so friendly. They had a little room off to the side of the kitchen; whack of course, but it had a chair and TV and they said I could stay as long as I wanted. It was so nice to sit and stare at a screen that I didn't even mind the flies. As usual, I couldn't finish my meal, but they said they would keep it in their refrigerator for me so I could eat it for breakfast. They made me feel as comfortable as possible until it was apparent it was time for me to go to bed. I was dreading it, but it had to be done. Just walk fast, get to your tent - you'll be fine.

I was almost through the parking lot when I saw them; two guys sitting on the decrepit lawn chairs in the dark. Oh, hell no. I turned right around to go back to my fly-infested hideout and stayed until it was painfully apparent it was time for me to go. I didn't know what I'd do if those guys were still there; I just prayed they had moved on. Except they were still there...only now they were putting up their tents. Oh, thank God! Not creepers, just hikers.

"Hopper" and "Big Cat" said a proper hello in the morning. Having them there allowed me to sleep without fear. They were both older like me, doing this midlife crisis/trying to find ourselves thing. Like many of the pairs I came across, they had found each other on the trail and formed a bond. As much as I loved seeing these friendships, I knew it was fated for me to be alone. My extreme slowness demanded it.

I made it to Native Landscapes just as they were opening. On top of retrieving the food I had sent myself, I needed to buy gas. The only reason I gave myself permission to dump mine out earlier was because my AT Guidebook specifically said that they carried it, along with a few other hiking supplies. Scanning the shelves in search of a container of white gas, I found only the canisters, which are useless for my stove. Why had I not considered this was the only type of gas they carried? I gave myself quite a scolding, not just for being so stupid as to think this place would actually sell white gas, but that I wasted half mine in the first place. Nothing to do now except hope I had enough until I could find more. Karma is such a bitch.

As soon as I was back on the AT, the rain came back with a vengeance. In this stretch, the shelters are closer together, so

I came to one that I didn't intend to stay at, and used it instead as a reprieve from the rain. A few other hikers were already in there doing the same thing, including Little Debbie. Maybe it was because she really didn't like me as I thought, or maybe she felt embarrassed smoking pot in front of an elder, but the air in the shelter was not only stinky - it was also horribly tense.

It was a relief when "Birdman" showed up. An "elder" like me, and also a section hiker, he was much more open to chat for a while. When you are around the thru-hikers, you can feel the need to defend your hiking prowess, so he was sure to explain that he was doing a "long ass section" that was nearly complete.

"You are going to want to get rid of those boots," he admonished. "I used to have boots too, but they are just useless in all this water. Trail runners are so much better. All the thru-hikers use them."

"Well, la dee freakin da," was what I was thinking, but instead just nodded in agreement. He asked where was I finishing and ending, so I told him.

"That's a longer section than me!" he said in a way that seemed more threatened than impressed. Either way, it was the most acknowledgment I'd gotten so far, so I should have felt flattered. But as much as I wanted to feel that way, I didn't. The air turned tense again.

Birdman decided it was time to brave the downpour, but the rest of us stayed, hoping it would let up a little. Instead, it picked up. Finally, I relinquished to the drencher; it wasn't like it was possible to get any wetter anyway.

I found my destination of Ten Mile Shelter to be a nest of men. Two sets of fathers and sons were keeping out of the rain and had taken it completely over; and lo and behold, Birdman was tucked in a corner as well. I teased that it was a bit too much of a party for me to handle, and in lieu of squeezing in between them, would be setting up my tent out back.

In rain like that, you click into a groove of gettin' er' done. You become a hyper-focused machine of efficiency. Being in this altered state, Birdman appeared, asking if I needed help. I know I wasn't rude, but I assured him I was good, even when he persisted in his attempts to be my knight.

"I created an extra hook in the shelter for you to use for your pack," he informed me.

"Oh, thank you, that was really nice, but I prefer to keep my stuff in my tent with me," I explained as graciously as I could while in my intensely hurried mode.

He departed in a huff, or at least it seemed that way to me...and that's when I got irritated. Of course, I appreciate help from others, but when you get offended just because someone is okay without it, you had better check yourself.

And here is where you will find the opening into bickering between a liberal and conservative mindset; my own divisive voices arguing to state their cases. The part of me that tells me he only wanted to be helpful, and I'm only being bitchy to think otherwise, and the part of me that is fighting to acknowledge what I feel (even if it makes me appear bitchy) are frequently at odds.

I grew up in a home where "feminist" was a dirty word. My mother was extremely proud to be a stay at home mom, and her aversion to the movement was not insistence on self-sabotage, but genuine love and pride in her role as wife and mother. She was traditional, and I guess what you would call conservative, though she was about as far from puritanical as someone could get. Like most humans, she was a beautiful mix of contradictions. And so I grew up knowing my role and did not question it.

My parents' relationship worked, and in no way did I ever see my mother as weak or lesser. My conservative self and upbringing is something I cherish, and I am grateful for the stability and safety that having your world grounded in absolutes provided.

And then there is my liberal self. Born from fire and pain, she arose from the ashes of my absolutes being destroyed. "Liberal" was the dirtiest word of all from my upbringing, and so this new self scared the crap out of me - mostly because I thought she would steal my faith. She didn't, but that is too long a story for little ol' chapter six. Though I will say that letting go of the absolutes I thought were faith, and opening up instead to absolute love, was the scariest, yet best thing that could have happened to both my conservative and liberal selves.

As far as my "role" here at this moment in the rain filled woods, all I can say is I believe it was a step forward for me to refuse help. Not because I needed to prove anything or emasculate someone trying to be chivalrous, but simply because I didn't need or want it. And being annoyed with Birdman was okay too, though I did try to give him the grace we all need for being a human with an ego.

Even though it's true that women are not treated as equal to men in this world, another truth is 95% of the men I encountered during my 50 days did treat me as an equal, and related to me simply as a fellow sojourner. There is very little room for "roles" when you are on the trail because everyone is out there trying to do the same thing - keep going until the end while enjoying the journey as much as possible. Shouldn't that be how we always live? Maybe it's true that in the end - whether male or female, conservative or liberal, black or white, gay or straight - we are all just walking each other home.

NEEDING GAS IN MY TANK

The AT shelters are exactly what they claim to be and nothing more; a place to get out of the rain. Most are a lean-to design with three walls, overhanging roof, and room for about six hikers to sleep on the wood floor. If you are lucky they will have a fire pit or picnic table, sometimes even a porch type area, and very occasionally a loft, or even bunk beds like at RPH. Ten Mile Shelter had none of these things. It did provide a little extra space under the overhanging roof where you could fit your stove and cook with a little protection from the rain, without feeling like you were actually in the shelter amongst the sleeping bags and sweaty men.

As I stood there trying to get my stove to work so I could have a warm dinner, I disclosed I was almost out of gas. I couldn't help noticing one of the dads was also using a "real" stove, and yes, I was hoping he would offer me a little of his fuel. They explained they were locals, taking a few days to enjoy the trail, and unfortunately had nothing extra to spare.

"How do you all know each other?" I asked as I tried to stay focused on what I was doing at the same time. I sure didn't need a repeat of my last stove lighting failure; just the thought of it was making me extremely nervous. These guys would laugh me right out of their den...if I didn't burn them alive first, that is.

"We don't know each other; we just happened to have

picked the worst weekend this summer to take a trip with our sons," they joked.

Telling me their stories, the older man and his son with disabilities intrigued me the most. It was obvious Dave and Adam had a special bond. The extra care Dave took in administering his son's medication was just one of the things that impressed me. I was humbled by their strong determination to embrace life, regardless of its challenges.

Dave had some advice for me when he found out I had their same itinerary for the next few days. Apparently, a water crossing was coming up that was sure to be running too high if the rain kept up like it was supposed to.

"There's a two mile detour you'll need to take. Of course, you can go down to the stream and see if you can cross, but I highly doubt you'll be able to," he warned. He also went on to explain that he didn't know if they would actually make it to said water hazard, or any of their planned shelters stays either.

"Adam loves to hike, and he will go and go, but when the trail is super rocky like these sections are, he struggles with his balance. It really slows us down," he related.

I tried to pay attention, but honestly, I was still stuck on the water crossing information. Extra miles?! No...I was going to avoid that at just about any cost; so I was already thinking about attempting it, even if it meant swimming.

The rain continued on into the morning, which was miserable, so I made a quick departure as soon as I woke up. The man hive was still dormant when I made my exit, so I left without saying goodbye, which always feels rude. Though thankfully it wouldn't be the last I'd see of Dave and Adam.

Almost to my destination for the day, I made my last stop for water. As I was checking my phone and starting my last mile obsession routine with Guthook's, three southbound hikers stopped at the creek as well. The sun had come out, and the humidity was off the charts. The three young men had obviously become good friends on the trail, and listening to their playful verbal sparring brightened my mood.

"Spork, you really need to get more water. You never drink enough. I seriously don't know how you are not dehydrated," scolded one of them - sounding a lot like myself with my kids.

"Whatever. With all this moisture in the air, I think I'm just absorbing it in through my pores," came the sarcastic retort - sounding a lot like my kids.

In chimes the third, "I don't think it works that way. Quite the opposite, actually. Just drink more water, you cheese nug."

At some point, I interrupted their banter to ask if they knew much about the upcoming town. I was completely out of gas now and knew Kent was my best shot at finding some. They let me know they did see a small outdoor supply shop on the main street leaving town. When I informed them I was looking for white gas, I got the cringe face.

"From the looks of the outside, I don't think they would have much more than your basic supplies," was the discouraging news from Ollie. Unfortunately, I didn't see that I had much choice other than to try.

I arrived at the Mt. Algo Shelter at 5:00 pm, making my best time yet. I hated not pushing forward to make up miles while I still had so much daylight left, but it made the most sense for me to camp here so I could go into town without my 35-pound backpack. After claiming a good tent site, I dug out my lightweight day pack and filled it with chargers, credit cards, and my now empty MSR fuel bottle. My first visit to an actual town was only a mile away.

Kent is a quaint little place. Passing the cemetery, the school, the local five and dime, it all felt more like a movie set than a real town. As I approached Backcountry Outfitters, I agreed it looked far more like a tourist trap than any kind of sporting goods store.

"Yep, I'm screwed," I thought when I walked in and the first thing I saw was an ice cream counter and giant blackboard sign promoting the flavor of the day. A quick scan of the shelves proved all suspicions true - this place was more about selling "The Mountains are Calling" tee-shirts than any real gear. I was thankful I brought my fuel bottle with me because instead of buying a can of white gas as I had hoped, I would have to resign to plan B of filling it up with actual gas from the station across the street. I knew it was risky and had the potential of ruining my stove, but I had no alternative. Just before I left, I decided I really should at least ask.

"Can I have some gas with my Rocky Road?"

Okay, I didn't actually say that, but it is how stupid I felt asking. The guy at the counter didn't skip a beat; he just pointed me across the room and told me to see Steve. Thankfully I had my bottle with me because Steve picked up a giant can he had behind the counter and simply filled me up. He said to take it back to the ice cream counter with a dollar and some change, and I'd be good. Who'd a thought I could get my gas with a Rocky Road after all?

I chose to eat dinner at my first sit down restaurant only because I wanted to charge all my stuff for as long as possible. I brought three chargers for this purpose if you can believe that, because I can't. Three chargers on a trek where to save weight I didn't even take three underwear - that's priorities for you. I had my phone of course, but also my ancient iPod shuffle and a portable power bank, and I planned on charging them all up at the same time. Unfortunately, the only table with a couple of outlets nearby was in the bar, far too close to regular people for comfort. Their comfort, that is.

I stunk. A whole lot. It really was not nice of me to sit in any proximity to others, but as I mentioned earlier, this hike was turning me into a bit of an ass. I did at least apologize to the waitress for my stench. She laughed it off; she sees hikers all the time. It's no wonder - over 4000 people signed up to complete the hike in 2017. Businesses like this one must invest in a lot of air fresheners.

I couldn't help listening to the conversation going on amongst the locals who were bellied up to the bar. My ears perked up, especially since they were talking about news in my home state.

"Who takes a joyride on an airplane?" one man quipped. "What a nut job."

"Yeah, it's crazy. All this airline security, and then a ground crew worker just hops in and takes off," chipped in another. "And it's not like the Seattle airport is some rinky-dink place."

It was weird to be hearing about the airport that I flew out of just 11 days prior. Stranger still was getting a message that night from my sister in law saying she got stuck in the air for hours coming home from California because "They closed Seatac! Mechanic stole a plane!" Later she went on to add her son even knew him from his church, and nobody suspected he had any mental health issues. Turns out it really wasn't a joy ride, but an intentional last ride. Suddenly the mockery at the bar seemed so callus. It is far too easy to ridicule what we don't understand.

As I lay in my tent that night with my melancholy thoughts about life and death, I told myself I really needed to get up and get some water before it got too dark. Typically I would have done this already for my night's culinary requirements, but because of my excursion into town, I didn't have the need. But now I was thirsty...and cozy in my sleeping bag, lacking any desire to move in the slightest.

"For the love of God, why can't they build these shelters closer to the brooks? And why does the water always have to be down a steep hill? I've hiked all day and just want a damn drink," I bitched and moaned to myself while struggling out of my bag and into my shoes. Grabbing my Sawyer water filter, I trudged all the way there in a real mood. I kicked myself for not bringing my headlamp, being it was now pretty dark, and I was struggling to fill up my water bags. Just as I was about to mutter a few more curse words, I saw some headlamps coming toward me.

"Hey, you guys made it!" I cheered as Dave and Adam very slowly approached.

"Today is a new record. Fourteen hours of almost nonstop hiking. But yes, we made it," Dave answered in tired, delayed spurts.

I slinked back to my tent shamefaced but resolved to embrace this adventure with a little less bellyaching, and a lot more gratitude.

THE JOYS OF BODILY FUNCTIONS

Day 12 brought with it a case of the squirts. Yes, I'm starting to repeat myself. Hiking is like that. Same shit over and over. (Ba-dum chhhh...)

Hiking Lingo Term #7 Privy: A toilet located in a small shed outside; an outhouse. Not to be confused with a backwoods toilet, which is a box in the open air with a toilet seat on top of it.

Having to use mostly backwoods toilets while hiking in Washington, I was so thankful for the nicer than usual privies that Connecticut offers at the shelters. Though, I sure regretted not getting a tent spot a little closer to the one at Mt. Algo. I'll confess that I didn't even make it the first time my dreaded bodily function issue arose. I barely made it behind the closest tree.

Thank God it was the middle of the night because I was far from alone. At least 10 tents were scattered about, and I had to pass most of them in a rush to not soil myself about four times before daylight. I thought maybe the waitress was so offended at my boldness to contaminate her section of tables with my funk that she spit in my food, or maybe my Sawyer water filter was not doing its job...either way, it was a problem. Nothing to be done about food poisoning, but I could order a new water filter. The miracle of Amazon had it waiting for me when I reached my first homestay, but let's not get ahead of ourselves. I still need to finish crappy day 12.

I know the last chapter concluded with my resolve to be more positive and less of a crybaby, but that lasted for all of about an hour. A second bodily function issue was upon me, and it was ratcheting up the cranky factor considerably. Yep, you guessed it - Aunt Flow had reared her ugly head. Damn her. She about did me in on that nine day hike I keep referring back to, and so I thought I would outsmart her and start the pill a few weeks before I left. I must say it was the best thing I did to prepare for this odyssey and helped immensely with my period; taming it to a manageable amount, instead of my usual premenopausal torrent.

Needless to say, it was a long night, and once I took my last run to the toilet after breakfast, I was ready to say good riddance to Mt. Algo and it's nicer than usual privy. As soon as I was all packed up, "Slim Jim" came up to me to give me some hiking advice. I met him the day before, cranky himself because he was just coming back on the trail after taking a few days hiatus, and during our small talk, I had mentioned how slow I was.

"Cowbell, I think your problem is your stride is too short. You really should try to take bigger steps," he counseled.

"Oh no, it's not Cowbell, it's Kellbell. Like in Kelly," I corrected him. Nicely too, in spite of myself.

"Kellbell? Is that because Kelly is your real name? Too bad it's not Cowbell. That actually would have been a cool name."

I resisted the urge to give him a cow kick to the shin and somehow managed a forced smile instead. I also withheld any snarky comeback about what a clever name Slim Jim was, and left his chubbiness out of it. I would rather pretend nice than be honestly rude, even if it makes me a bit of a fake. Though sometimes I wish I was more genuine, and I'm often jealous of those who can say exactly what they feel. But, me being me, I only demonstrated my attempt at a longer gait...then took them straight away from Slim Jim, along with a few mutterings under my breath.

It was beginning to rain again when I passed Dave and Adam. I believe Adam is non-verbal, though I could be wrong; but he gave a big smile when I asked if I could take their picture. I congratulated them again on their amazing accomplishment of 14 hours of hiking and confessed that the few times I managed to pull off 13 it just about killed me. Dave let me know with the rain coming on they would not be attempting to descend Saint John Ledges, but instead would be going off the trail. I wished them well and went on my way. I would later scold myself for not asking more questions about these mysterious "ledges," but at the time I thought little of it.

When I reached the ledges in question, it was dumping buckets. I later discovered this is an area climbers like to use, so the trail was at its steepest yet. And by "trail," I mean the typical AT pile of rock, though these ones were particularly large and difficult to maneuver down, not to mention extremely slippery. I was not having fun, and let's just say that my attitude could have been better.

Finally, at the bottom, I came to a gravel road and praised the heavens that I had some flat miles ahead. A bit of a disgruntled laud, due to the sudden onslaught of mosquitoes (you'd think the downpour would slow them down a little) but still a slight improvement from my overall dour mood. The double blaze at the road intersection showed I should turn right, being the right stripe was higher than the other. I didn't bother double-checking with my phone because I didn't want to get it wet; and besides, it was obvious. Even though it took me the first few days to decipher the reason for the double blazes, once I did, I found them consistent and helpful.

It was quite a while before I noticed I hadn't seen another blaze. Typically you don't get many once you are on a road; but still, I should have seen at least one. Annoyed, I thought I'd better dig out my phone and make sure because I really didn't need another reason to hate this day. And sure enough, my dot was way off the trail. Expletives in abundance. When I got back to the double blaze, I took a hard look, because what the hell. Then I realized that the angle of the blazes was more in line with what a south bounder would be looking at, directing them to the place they needed to get off the road and turn right up the hill. I gave another meager offering of thanks that at least I was now headed in the right direction, and surrendered to the idea that I would call it quits when I reached the very next shelter.

Gaucho, Skeeter, and of course, Little Debbie were all hanging out in the Stewart Hollow Shelter when I arrived. The rain was still coming down hard, and for the first time, I felt cold - and not just because of Little Debbie. I really wanted to put on dry clothes, and more importantly, deal with my increasingly urgent feminine hygiene situation; but I just couldn't bear going out in the rain to put up my tent.

I knew I could go looking for the privy or go hide behind a tree to deal with the hygiene issue - it's not like I hadn't done that plenty already - but that still left me in soaking wet clothes. Even if I did try to change in the privy, (which you know was never going to happen) I would be drenched by the time I got back to the shelter; that is how hard it was raining. Then I remembered someone had told me that hikers will often put up their tents in the shelters if there is room (I must have been telling them my RPH story) so like an idiot, I got the harebrained idea that this was going to be a good plan.

"If there is room" is kind of a major component I was leaving out of this equation, but desperate times call for desperate measures. I honestly think this was the smallest shelter ever, with three people already huddled in one corner; and here I was trying to put up a tent that was at least a half foot too long to even set on the floor. Once I got going though, there was no stopping me. With an unappreciative audience looking on, I somehow got it together enough to barely stay upright. Taking up almost half the shelter, part of it hanging over the edge, the rain fly draped over haphazard like...it was a full-on ridiculous spectacle.

Sometime during this shit show Dave and Adam showed up; I think it was when I was getting my tent poles put together and the crew in the corner were trying their best not to get impaled. Picture this - a lance-like object that once assembled is eight feet long, and also has four feet long antennae protruding from one end. I'm afraid my "this tent is so small it will fit" calculations were WAY off.

"I don't think putting that up in here is a good idea," Dave cautioned in a very diplomatic fashion.

"YA THINK?!"

Of course, you already know I didn't actually say that, but I certainly was thinking it. I kept putting up the tent just the same. I knew at this point the tent was a bad idea, and that it was embarrassingly obvious to everyone; except I was deep enough in that I couldn't quit.

"It's still pretty early in the day. With this storm, we are bound to get more hikers wanting to stop and get out of the rain. You really should only put up a tent if there are only a couple people staying in it," he added to try and dissuade me. How was I supposed to answer? "Let me change my tampon and then I'll be out of your way?" I did feel bad, but I was also in full swing asshole mode and going to do what I needed to whether anyone liked it or not. This hike was indeed transforming me, but not quite in the way I had hoped for. Mumbling something about needing a few minutes, I crawled inside my tent and did my business, hoping nobody could see through the small gaps left by my atrociously hung rainfly. It was a low moment for sure.

Once I had taken my tent down and everyone could sit in the shelter as comfortable as possible, I had the chance to ask Dave and Adam why they were even there in the first place. How in the world did they get down that mountain, much less so fast?

"We took the shortcut," Dave nonchalantly explained as if I should know what he was talking about. "It just made sense in this weather."

No fair having the advantage of being a local. But it was probably a good thing I didn't ask him earlier what he meant by going off the trail, because if I knew there was a short cut, I most likely would have taken it. Though, it did get me thinking. My goal was hiking 500 miles within these five states...I never said they would all be on the AT. I already skipped one of those miles and ended up adding an extra three to four miles on the Red Dot Trail. I deduced this meant I had at least three miles in cheater chips I could use whenever I could; in fact, why not include the two miles I did when I went into Kent? Heck, I even did an extra mile today when I took that wrong turn. So the accumulation of about six miles thus far to not feel guilty about skipping, this was my verdict. I had five days until my homestay at Jess Treat's house, where I hoped to cash a few of those cheater chips in.

The truth was that making my 500 mile goal at all was looking more bleak every day. Stopping early yet again officially put me a whole three days behind. But I held tight to the hope that as long as I kept moving, I'd get faster, and slowly but surely eventually catch up. Plus finding ways to cheat a little always helps.

Slim Jim showed up just as the rain was letting up, so I decided it was time to give up my spot in the shelter and put up my tent again...this time outside, of course. As soon as I had my tent up and ready, Slim came over to tell me I'd better rethink my location.

"You should always look up before you decide where to put your tent. See that big branch right above you? I wouldn't trust it," he pointed out. I was thankful for his concern and wisdom, even if I was a touch aggravated by his know-it-all-ishness. I certainly wasn't happy with the prospect of finding a new spot, and I was almost pissy enough to stay put, even with the threat of a tree limb of death. But reason prevailed, and I went ahead and put up my tent a third time. Getting squashed by a widowmaker was not the cherry on top I needed for this crap pie of a day.

FEELING LUCKY

Waking up on day 13, all I could think was how glad I was day 12 was behind me. No killer tree limbs fell that night, but because my final tent spot was just feet from Slim Jim's hammock, I ended up having to hear him snore for the better part of the evening. It had been a bad day, pretty much from start to finish.

The one redeeming moment was seeing Lighting Rod again. He appeared out of nowhere when I was making dinner, sporting the new super-lightweight backpack that he had told me he was ordering the last time I saw him. Wondering how I could possibly be ahead of him with the pace I was going, he explained that when he picked up his pack in town, he ended up staying a few days, due to a bee sting on his foot that made it almost impossible to even walk. And wouldn't you know he had another grand tale about somebody letting him stay at their house...actually not just a house, but apparently a full-on mansion. Just a random guy he met, who when hearing that LR was a thru-hiker, offered him to come on over and have full reign of his crib while he was away on business. I don't think there is a woman out there that would have taken any man up on an offer like that, but great that it worked out for him.

As soon as he had told his tale, LR was off again. Too much daylight left, and too many miles to catch up on. I had miles on my mind too. No more stopping so early, I told myself. Going over my AT Guide before bed that night, I came up with a new plan to make up miles. Twelve miles should not be that hard. And if I could keep it up, I'd be caught up in a couple of weeks.

Tomorrow was a new day.

I didn't get the early start I was hoping for, and only Dave and Adam were left when I said my goodbyes. It would be the last time I saw them, and I was appreciative of Dave's final directives about how to avoid the upcoming water crossing of doom, even though I was pretty sure I wasn't going to heed them.

"Today is looking better already," I thought to myself as the sun made her appearance. Before I knew it, I was at the road where the sign was posted warning of the high running creek below, along with a map of where the two miles of road walking would get you back on the trail. Should I be smart and stay on the road, or risk it and head down? I decided I should at least go take a look; I could always turn around.

Hiking Lingo Term #8 Ford: Crossing a stream or river where it is shallow enough to traverse by wading.

Dave failed to mention how steep and long it was getting down to the stream from the road, so my considerations of playing it safe were now out the window. This was do-or-die. I was feeling lucky, but I didn't like the look of the place where the trail was supposed to cross the fast moving stream. Even though there were rocks to step on, enough water was passing over them to make it look extremely treacherous; especially with the drop off that you would be sure to go over if you slipped. So I bushwhacked a little upstream and found a place that looked doable, and though it was definitely the deepest ford I've ever done, it was nowhere near swimming. Climbing up the bank on the other side was the most difficult part, but then I was golden.

As I was putting my shoes back on, I was feeling pretty proud of myself - until another group of guys started to cross. The leader of their pack had a dog on a leash, and he barely hesitated before charging forward over the slippery rocks like there was nothing to it; with his dog pulling him forward even! I watched in disbelief; in fact, I even looked away at one point,

I was so anxious about him going over the edge. I could tell the other guys were not so sure about the sanity of this plan of action but followed only because they didn't want to look like wussies. I even wonder if they all went across so boldly because they saw me sitting there and figured it couldn't be that bad. And it wasn't. So much for my pride.

My luck ran out at about 5:00 pm. No disaster, I just came to a stop. I don't know what to say, except I was too tired to go on. It felt like this day had been nothing but steep hills, and somehow always seemingly up instead of down. Lightning Rod had bolted by me a couple of times, and each time I watched him march up the hill in a quarter of the time it would take me, another part off of my hiker soul would break. I would eventually crawl to the top, and there he'd be, always with a few others - resting, smoking, laughing. As much as I wanted to hate the lot of them, I couldn't. Their youthful exuberance and ease with life was a joy to see. Puppies...that is what they reminded me of. Except for you-know-who...she was more like grumpy cat.

"Cowbell, don't you worry. You'll get your hiker legs soon," they would cheer me on as I inched by them. Sometimes I could hear LR delicately correcting them once I passed, "Her name is Kellbell." Another reason why he was my favorite. Three weeks time and these magical legs would arrive; that's what they were telling me. Stopping early today, yet again, with my mile deficit compounding daily, all I could think was...they'd better. With one more week of this degree of slowness while waiting for my upgrade, they'd better be frickin' superhuman hiker legs or I was absolutely not going to make it to Ethan Pond on foot. Make no mistake, I knew I would get there somehow, save a hospital stay or death; but I really wanted to get there in the way I intended.

This is part of the grand plan I have yet to expound on, but first I'll need to tell you about Leigh. In 2014 Leigh came with me on her very first backpack; actually, I think it was her first time in a tent. I was shocked when she said she wanted to come.

I hardly knew her, but in my estimation, she didn't seem the type. (The fact she brought mascara being a possible confirmation...I'll never let her live that down.) Once we were on the trail, being with her was like being with a kid at Disneyland who has never been; she fell head over heels with hiking that hard. Though, how could she help it? It was a jaw dropping trip to nearly the highest point on the PCT in Washington at the climax of the fall colors. Only one night, perfect weather, maybe five miles total in and out; there was nothing not to love. She then informed me she wanted to come with me on the following year's seven day outing on Section J - one of the toughest sections on the PCT, and one that allows for no good escape route if you suddenly decided hiking wasn't for you. Was Leigh truly in love, or just infatuated? I wasn't sure, but seven days of mosquitoes, rain, and foot destroying talus would certainly reveal the truth. I was more than a little nervous to find out.

Hiker Lingo Term #9 Talus: Large, loose broken stones on the side of a mountain, or an area covered with stones.

When we were on our next to last day on Section J, Leigh turned around to ask me, "What do you call all this rock again? If I'm going to curse at it, I want to call it by its proper name." Even with all the horrible miles of talus Section J provided, Leigh proved herself a beast on that trip. Her tenacity, wit, and the pissed off grunting noises she makes when she's frustrated have made her one of my favorite people. We have hiked together every year since then, and there was no way in hell she was going to miss doing a few days on the AT with me.

So after exhaustive planning - arranging and rearranging flights, booking buses, rental cars, and separate rooms at the Joe Dodge Lodge - everything was in place for her to come along with Ken and join me. After almost six hours of flying, then six more of driving, and then two more of hiking, they would rendezvous with me at the campsite on Ethan Pond, and then finally we would all hike together for my last four days in the White Mountains. So whether by my miraculously enhanced hiking limbs or by a call to an Uber driver, greeting Ken and Leigh on day 46 was non-optional.

> *Hiking Lingo Term #10 Stealth: The term given to setting up your tent in an unestablished site. Stealth sites are typically not noted in any guidebooks, making them impossible to plan for.*

For all my resolve to make up miles, I couldn't keep moving on this not so lucky after all day of 13. When I found a stealth spot next to a small creek, I called it quits. A few tears mixed in my quick meal, and I was in bed by 6:00 pm. With my rally cry of "tomorrow's a new day" stuck in my throat, I was asleep by 6:05.

Despite my having it plugged in, I awoke to a dead phone. Like an alcoholic's empty bottle, it caused me great panic. How do I live without it? My hope was that the power bank was just empty, although it seemed like with the long charge I was able to give it at the restaurant only three days prior, it should have some juice left. I couldn't deal with the thought of my phone being actually broken, and focused instead on finding a place I could spend a good while charging it; preferably without angering any restaurant staff. Scanning my book, I found a note saying there was a place to charge that was open to hikers at a strange sounding shed just outside of Falls Village.

"Covered in vines" was the clue I had, and when I came upon the small, junky, garage type structure, I saw other hikers laying down in the yard and figured I was in the right place. Asking them if they knew where the outlets were, they kind of shrugged indifferently and said they supposed I should just go inside. Obviously, they were not concerned about their phones.

It felt strange to wander inside an unknown building filled with miscellaneous clutter and hijack a stranger's power, but I was extremely pleased to see the little bolt icon cheerfully appear once I did. "It's alive!"...I was so relieved. Now to kill some time while it fully recovers. Humm, maybe I should exercise my social skills and talk to those other hikers. Ugh.

I always tried to get people's trail names, but I somehow missed theirs, so I'll name the couple myself: "The European Snobs." I'm sorry, I don't mean to add to any nasty stereotypes; almost every other European I met had been lovely. But the impression these two were giving me was that acknowledging my presence was not worth the effort. I made my presence known anyway and asked them some questions. They were thru-hikers as I suspected, and when I told them I was doing 500 miles, his response was, "So this is like a little vacation for you?" (Be sure to read that with a pretentious sounding accent.)

"And it's not for you? Did I misunderstand, or is someone paying you to do this? I didn't know you were professional hikers - wow, congrats."

I'm finding it quite satisfying writing out the mean sarcastic thoughts that I never say out loud. It's therapeutic, but also a bit alarming to see I'm not the nicey nice person I like to think I am. Maybe the trail wasn't turning me into an ass...maybe it was just revealing that I already was one. Anyway, after I did my awkward laugh like "that was a good one!" I continued with some more self-deprecation about how slow and behind I was, because at least it made for conversation.

"You really need to lose those boots. For every gram you lose off your feet, it equals five off your back," he informed me in a condescending fashion.

"Sorry, you lost me at gram. Me dumb American." I wanted to say it but instead changed the subject to my phone and how glad I was that it wasn't broken. "I don't know what I'd do without my phone. Being alone, I really rely on it. I mean, what if a fell and twisted my ankle?"

"You don't need a phone. There are enough people on this trail that someone would be by to help you in 15 minutes or less," he quickly rebutted.

Then in quipped Mrs. European Snob, "And besides, you could never twist your ankle in those giant boots of yours," and they both had a good little patronizing chuckle.

Okay, enough with the social interaction exercise. After one last "Oh you guys are hilarious" fake laugh, I was out of there. I thought I should check out the "outdoor shower" mentioned that was somewhere on the side of the building, and after a quick cold rinse off (yes, with clothes on, of course. You are never dry with all the humidity anyway) I sat to contemplate what to do next. I still had around four hours of daylight, so continuing on would be the smartest move. But I knew a town was less than a half mile away...and the notes said camping is allowed at the Toy Maker's Cafe...and cafe means food...and to hell with catching up, it's probably hopeless anyway...

Time to try my luck in Falls Village.

PAY IT FORWARD

My AT Guide's instructions were to go to the back of the building and knock on the resident's upstairs apartment if the Toy Maker's Cafe was closed, which it was. How odd. This was someone's house - someone who obviously lets complete strangers stay in their backyard. Who does that? Plus it seemed a little...can I say whack again? The graffiti covered van parked out back was kind of giving it that feel. I headed up the stairs anyway.

A very sweet woman greeted me and gave me the quick rundown: Don't trample the plants, if you get water from the hose be sure to turn it off because it floods the basement, feel free to use the electrical outlets on the side of the barn, the cafe opens at 7:00 am. I tried to give her a little money for the tent site, but she wouldn't hear of it. Pay it forward, she said. I know there are many ways to be generous, but the thought of letting anybody come and park it on my lawn made me realize that this lady and I were on completely different levels of kindness. I was pretty sure my pay it forward was going to suck in comparison.

I wanted to get going really early in the morning, but how could I leave before the cafe opened and miss out on the food? Why not wait - there might be eggs benedict on the menu, and does a late start really even matter anymore? And then terror suddenly struck me...there is no bathroom available until 7:00 am! Except for those couple of episodes of diarrhea, my pooping schedule was set in stone; 6:00 am, and there was no stopping it. The horrible truth settled in. I was going to have to take a shit in this nice lady's backyard. That was most definitely not paying it forward.

I obsessed about it all night, and for the life of me could not come up with a solution except to pre dig a good hole way back behind the barn. As discreetly as possible, I snuck back there with my shovel to check it out. It was clear this was an area for compost, so heck, maybe I was paying it forward after all! I got my hole ready for the morning and prayed that I wouldn't have to use it.

Sometime during the night, I was awoken by a commotion right next to my tent. Trying not to panic, I sat very still and just listened. Scattered curse words and the clicking of tent poles let me know it was just another hiker setting up next to me. From the safety of my sleeping bag I called out a greeting, "Hey there, I'm Kellbell. It's nice to have some company tonight. Crazy being here in these folk's backyard, huh?"

"Oh, yeah, hello...damn these tent poles. It's been a long day. Today is my four month anniversary on the trail. God, why does this tent have to be such a pain in the ass? (mumbled obscenities) Oh, my name's Close Call by the way."

I thought there must be quite a story behind that name, but instead of asking, I only wished her a good night's sleep. I could tell she was in no mood for chit chat, which I wouldn't be either after finishing at that hour.

By a miracle of the sphincter gods, I was able to hold it until 7:00 am. Thinking back now, I don't know why it didn't occur to me that using one of my plastic bags and packing it out as an option; that would have relieved me of all that stress. Though the stress was probably what saved me in the end (no pun intended).

The eggs benedict was so good I finished it all, left a good tip (which was a much better pay it forward than extra compost material) and headed back toward the trail. I wanted to say goodbye to Close Call, but she was still sound asleep when I left, poor thing. Oh well, as a thru-hiker, she'd be sure to blow by me within a few hours.

Except I never did see her that day. Plenty others passed me though like I was a tractor on a freeway. For some reason it did not bother me at all - maybe breakfast really is the most important meal of the day. When I reached the top of the first major hill, there was a huge convergence of people sitting on a big rock smoking and having a full on hiker festival. I was confused at first how there could be such a large group when I was sure only half that amount had passed me, but then I remembered the south bounders. I felt suddenly jealous at the ease of which extraverts can mingle with strangers as if they have been lifelong friends. If I had a cocktail maybe...wait, it's the pot! That would certainly help most people loosen up, though not me. I've only tried it once, and I swear I'm allergic or something. I doubted any of these folks wanted to deal with the deranged paranoia of someone who thought they could summon horrible realities with their mind or suspected they were already dead. No, I thought it best for everyone that I just keep moving.

I heard a voice as I was passing, "Hey Kellbell, you ready for that tattoo yet?" There sat For Now in the crowd with his blue hair and mischievous grin. With a laugh, I said I was not quite ready, but that I had told my youngest daughter we could get hummingbird tattoos when I got back to celebrate my 50 days and her 18th birthday.

"You should fly her out here! Two free tattoos would be worth the plane ticket. Plus, it would be a great experience for her. Hiking develops character!"

"I would probably push her off a cliff after three days," I thought. Don't get me wrong, I'm crazy about her; but an extended hiking trip together would certainly kill one of us...if not by each other's own hand, then possibly from hepatitis from a free trail tattoo.

I pulled off a little more small talk with the crowd and felt pretty accomplished considering my introvert bent, but taking off my pack and mingling any longer was just not going to happen. Only a few steps into my retreat and I took my second fall.

My first fall days earlier made sense; it was on a slippery decline where my feet just went out from under me. But this one came out of nowhere. I have no idea what happened; though understand that once your pack weight starts taking you, there is not much you can do. I toppled and tumbled like an out of control downhill skier through the sticker bushes, and as soon as I was done, hopped up with the adrenaline rush that only the fear of having others see your epic fail can provide. With a quick look behind me, I confirmed I was blessedly just out of sight of the group. Although I love to make others laugh, that was not the comedy show I wanted to provide. With the priority of making sure I did not make a mockery of myself out of the way, I could now check to see if I was actually hurt. Nope, just a few scratches, thank God.

Falling on the trail really ought to be fear #1, as it is the main reason for hiking deaths. (Technically it's drowning, though doesn't that always require a fall of some kind first?) I can't tell you how many times I've fallen, and occasionally, like this time, what even caused it. You can maneuver over all kinds of obstacles for days, and then have the tiniest shift of weight or unseen root take you down. I'll never forget the second day of that seven day trip with Leigh. Just enough miles in to make an injury more of a disaster than an inconvenience, and I was suddenly face down in the dirt. Leigh was ready to take off in search of help but then realized nothing was in fact wrong. No heart attack or brain aneurysm - I just fell for no apparent reason. We laughed of course because, apart from my pride, I was unhurt; and going over like a felled tree is a hysterical sight. Not so funny is the realization that this could happen when a precipice is involved, which is something you just have to put out of your mind.

"Pack Rat" was the next thru-hiker I would meet. Resting and taking a snack break, I went ahead and joined him, being I was feeling somewhat confident with my social savvy that day. He was older, which I think put me a little more at ease. We at least had that to talk about. When I told him I was just over two weeks on the trail and looking forward to getting my trail legs soon, he broke the unfortunate news that only the youngsters get legs at three weeks. My 50 year-old legs would take closer to six weeks to appear. Fanfuckingtastic. Making sure I still had the Uber app on my phone, I shuffled away in discouragement. Nothing to do but just keep going, with or without hiker's legs...or the hope of finishing this quest on foot.

And continue I did, up and up, and despite Pack Rat's let down, I felt stronger than ever. I pumped myself up with thoughts that I was good enough, smart enough, and doggone it, I could do this! (Stuart Smalley fans unite!) When I came to the dreaded Lion's Head Peak, I had the choice of going straight up another pile of rocks or taking the blue blaze detour. Breakfast must truly be the most important meal of the day because I charged up and over those rocks like a real thru-hiker.

Basking in my triumph at the top, I met a local named Brian who pointed out the sights below, like Twin Lakes and the Salisbury Ski Jump. Though the view was not much by Washington's standards, it was a beautiful day, and I tried to soak it all in for a few minutes at least. When Brian asked me where I was staying for the night, I said I was planning on skipping the upcoming shelter and pushing on to the next, even though it was getting late. As soon as we parted, my suspicious self started pestering me.

"Why did you tell him where you would be tonight? He knows you're alone - what if he's a psychopath? You just made yourself a great target, moron."

My sensible self was quick to intervene, "Seriously? You think some guy, with no gear whatsoever, is going to traipse through the woods for miles to try and find you, then hope he can escape down this mountain in the dark without killing himself? Geez, no wonder pot makes you paranoid. You are delusional as it is."

Though as soon as my fretful mind comes on, she is not easily quieted. With dusk on its way, I began getting jumpy. I started hearing things. At first, I tried to convince myself it was just my fear getting the best of me, but then I couldn't deny the distinct howling coming from very nearby. No way I was going any further. Following the signs leading me to the Riga Shelter, I consoled myself that though I was stopping short of my goal once again, I was at least throwing that local rapist off my trail. As I approached the shelter, I heard the howls very loudly - then suddenly saw the only animals making the ruckus were a group of kids; and yes, they were literally howling for fun.

It turned out to be a girl's youth group overnight outing; so even my fretful, delusional, paranoid self could continue to be worried anymore. Thus, although there was all the noise from the rambunctious preteens throughout the evening, it was my best night of sleep yet.

GIVE ME A BREAK

Another grind up a Bear Mountain, another boring view of rolling hills. Only 16 days in, and I was really starting to feel over it. Maybe it was my period, maybe homesickness - but most likely I legit needed a rest day.

This is something I did not think much about when I came up with this whole plan. I thought my 10 miles a day for 50 days should not be that big a deal, especially when in comparison to everyone else's supposed 20 mile a day average. What I did not consider is that everyone else takes rest days. And to make matters worse, I'm convinced they don't include rest days into their daily average, which is very misleading.

If I do 20 miles a day for six days, then don't hike at all on day seven, my average is no longer 20 miles a day, but 17.1, right? I am quite certain that the average hiker is doing nowhere near 20 miles a day on this trail, and wish I knew where I read that so I could vehemently declare it wrong. Every other person I talked to was doing closer to 15 miles a day, then taking rest days once a week or more. Not to mention doing at least a little slackpacking, which I'll explain more about later, but in a nutshell, it's hiking packless.

Unfortunately, if you have been told that everyone else can average 20 miles a day hauling 30+ pounds, then you assume you should at least be able to pull it off once or twice. And because I really did believe that at some point I'd pull a 20 here and there, I'd also be able to possibly sneak in a zero-day a couple of times at least. Obviously, this was not proving true in the slightest.

I knew my upcoming stay at Jess Treat's house could not be a full-on rest day, but at least it was a few hours away from the trail. Most importantly though, it would include a hot shower. I found her in my all-knowing guide book and had sent ahead my supplies with the ETA of August 15th. I texted her on the 12th letting her know I was behind schedule, then again on the 14th that I was really behind schedule.

"The AT is kicking my ass" is how I explained it, and when I said I hoped to get there on the 18th, she was sure to ask me if I was certain, because "those 20 miles from Salisbury are very difficult. Three mountains and a very technical descent." Who could blame her for doubting my abilities? But I was now obsessed with getting there ASAP.

When I told her I promised to be at the road pick up no later than 5:30 pm on the 18th, she texted back that it was her birthday, and she had plans for the evening.

"Perhaps a friend can get you," she suggested. Oh yeah, all my East Coast buddies, I'll go ahead and ring one up. What was she thinking? Thankfully she clarified the next day that it was one of her friends she was thinking of as a replacement driver and informed me she had it all worked out. "Papa Joe will be picking you up" was all I needed to know.

After coming down from Bear Mountain, I crossed into my third state. Massachusetts' Sages Ravine was the AT's shining moment thus far. This canyon has the most enchanting brook, with glistening pools and graceful waterfalls cascading into it. You get to walk right alongside it - sometimes going high to get perfect views down, and then going back low to feel intimately close and engulfed in its magic spell.

The bewitchment was suddenly broken when I passed the stunning Sages Ravine Campsite and remembered how carefully I had arranged my miles to make this my intended campsite for day 13 of my now completely fucked up agenda. Sigh...at least I had the right idea because this would have been the best camp of the whole trip. Chin up - I couldn't lament for long if I wanted to get to Papa Joe on time.

I passed the party crew, who were taking a dip in the stream's serene pools, and heard LR amongst the crowd, "Hey Kellbell, can you believe how amazing this is?" Oh, to be a puppy again. I smiled and agreed it was truly spectacular, but had to also tease him about our hare and tortoise dance, which I was now in the lead of.

"When you gonna get serious about finishing this hike?" I razzed. "If you keep going my pace, it's going to be snowing when you hit Mt Kardashian!" - which was more truth than taunting. He laughed and promised he'd be finishing, though to this day I don't know if he did or not. I might not ever know, considering I never asked his real name.

I reminded myself I had until 5:30 pm the next night to make it to the Route 7 crossing for my pick up. In fact, I reminded myself about every five minutes. It's all I could think about. If I could push up and over this last mountain, it would be a cruise the following day, and maybe I could get Papa Joe to pick me up early and have almost a half day to rest at the house. Fantasies, all fantasies. The other app I had downloaded to assist me was called Appalachian Trail Weather, and it was warning me of an upcoming storm. That was all I needed to grant my whiney self permission to stop a little early for the day, with the hopes my stronger self could pull up the slack and get a full 10 miles the next day.

Sometimes your whiney self is a lifesaver because the storm that hit was a doozy. I was thankful for the safety of my tent, but the early night gave me far too much time to feel forlorn. Desperate for some company, I sent out a few texts, looking for a bite. "Just a lonely girl in a tent, looking for some news"...then a response from a friend, "Hey girl!"

Heather and I texted back and forth for quite a while;

talking about our teenage girls and their volleyball struggles, her foster son accidentally using all their data in one day, and having to put her dog down. Real life stuff. Was I out here to escape real life? What did I think I'd find? I know what I found at that moment; the truth that I needed people. Life is precious, even with it's dying dogs and family stress. It's those hardships that bond us together; they are the very things that give us empathy and opportunity to care for and love each other. And even though this trail was not my normal life, I had to acknowledge it was still very much real life. This pain was teaching me - it's good to reach out, it's good to be vulnerable, and it's good to long for company because it makes me human. And even though this little interaction with Heather was short and not face to face, it was enough. It had to be because I had to save some charge on my phone to contact Papa Joe the next day. I couldn't wait.

My final obstacle of Mt. Everett proved to be as horrible as the Guthook's elevation profile's sharp spike made it seem. This was another wonderful/horrible feature of this app - being able to look ahead to see exactly how much of an elevation gain or loss you were about to suffer. Cresting the peak and now almost down the other side, a thunderstorm suddenly came on hard, and my patience ran out completely. I was so done with the slippery granite sloping rocks, and I said so very loudly and with much conviction...along with several curse words for added emphasis. Out from the forest ahead came a voice, "You having a bad day?"

"Oh geez, I'm sorry. I didn't see you there. Yes, I'm having a bad moment. I'm so over these rocks," I confided to the approaching hiker.

"I've been cursing the mosquitoes all day. It's like the rain just stirs them up. I'm ready to climb some rocks just to get away from them. If it makes you feel better, you won't be dealing with rocks for awhile. But what you are about to face is what the locals call mosquito alley," was his not so encouraging encouragement. And though the bugs were as plentiful as promised, I blew through there so fast they didn't have a chance to chomp. Most times when I was facing a mosquito infested area, I was going up a steep hill, making me feel like a plate of sushi on one of those slow moving conveyor belts. But not this day. I may not have had my hiker legs yet, but my acute desire for a hot shower was its own superpower.

When I, at last, broke free from the green tunnel and hit a gravel road, I found no blaze, sign, or indicator whether I should go right or left. My book said to go “west," which might as well have been in Chinese with my sense of direction; plus I was officially suddenly at the end of my paid maps, causing my Guthook's app to once again be of no use. I know it's crazy, but I was on the fence about buying more. I'm that cheap for real; plus I did want to try and free myself from my addiction. I saw a road to my right, and even though I was pretty sure it was not the designated Route 7, I headed toward it anyway. I knew I most likely had another mile to where I was supposed to be, but I was ready to cash in one of my chips. I called Papa Joe with the little charge I had left and described where I was, and he said he'd be there in about 15 minutes.

I was feeling very excited, relieved, nervous - all at the same time. What if Papa Joe is creepy? What if this is all some scam to abduct me and sell me into the sex trade? These thoughts pop up, and even though my logical brain knows how unlikely they are, the fact that they are not 100% impossible makes it difficult for me to completely ignore them. (Well, it might be 100% improbable for a 50 year-old, but you can never be sure.)

Papa Joe turned out to be an angel. (Folks who help hikers are called "trail angels," though he seemed more of a literal angel to me.) He brought me free Gatorade and asked me questions about my journey. When he got out his notebook, I got a little freaked out again, but he quickly explained he documented every hiker he helps. He keeps a record of statistics about things like solo or not, female or male, southbound or northbound. I swear he only does this because he enjoys it. Retired and wanting to keep busy, this is how he chooses to spend his summer.

Sometimes it's hard to believe there are people without ulterior motives doing loving things in this world, but I promise you it's true. It saddens me that most of us are so suspicious, but I get it. If it is hard for me, a soul who has never been horribly taken advantage of, then I know it's near impossible for those who have been seriously hurt. But we lose so much when we live life with our dukes up, always expecting the worst in people. I'm not judging anyone who does so; self-protection is our biggest instinct for a reason. But sometimes I wonder if it does us more harm than good...I really do.

I let Papa Joe take my picture for his Instagram page, but he would not let me give him a cent for the ride. I thanked him profusely, then nervously approached the house; though because I somehow managed to get my 10 miles in a little before 5:30, Jess was just leaving for her birthday party and opened the door before I could even knock.

"Oh wow, you got here early. The guys will explain everything to you; they are sitting in the living room. I believe you already know one of them," she quickly informed me as she ran out the door. I was so overwhelmed with the odd feeling of being in a stranger's home, on the opposite coast from everything I knew and in a situation that was completely foreign to me, that my mind could not even fathom how anything familiar could be sitting in the next room.

"Well, isn't it something seeing you here! How is it going, Pack Rat?"

I was so glad I was able to recall his name...I didn't need another Little Debbie situation on my hands. We said our hellos, and the other hiker introduced himself as a southbounder named "Too Many." When Pack Rat teased, "Is that in reference to your relatives?", Too Many soberly explained that it was for the soldiers who have died in Afghanistan in battle, or by suicide after their return home. He went on to explain that this hike was a platform for him to speak and educate people, which is, of course, an inspiring and beautiful objective. Though with his slow southern drawl and gift of gab, I found myself antsy and anxious for my long awaited shower but feeling too guilty to interrupt. Graciously, Pack Rat did it for me.

"You really should get your shower," he suddenly announced with an abrupt matter-of-factness. Then it clicked - I am unequivocally radiating stink into this lovely room.

"Oh my God, you guys are dying, aren't you? I'm so sorry, I actually forgot what I smell like. Yes, yes, of course, I will clean up right now," I blabbered as I scampered about collecting my stuff, and rushed up the stairs to make my indelicate escape.

The indoor shower has to be one of the top inventions of the 19th century. It's something we all take for granted, but if you haven't had one in a couple of days (or in my case, weeks) you realize that it is actually a portal into Nirvana. I might say the same thing about a good mattress, or a fresh pot of coffee. I could write a whole book on suffering and never bring any of us into peace about its existence, but I can tell you one thing I know for sure; suffering makes you appreciate not suffering on a whole new level.

After my heavenly half hour in the bathroom, I retreated to my room to find all my treasures laid out on the bed. Amazon packages, including new headphones that I was sure would not arrive in time, the box of food and supplies I had sent ahead, and also loaner clothes from Jess that I could put on so that I could wash all my nasty gear at once and feel clean while doing it. I felt like a kid on Christmas morning. The only thing missing was loved ones to share it with.

As much as I wanted company, the thought of going back downstairs only carried with it a weight. There is a gravity to opening up to strangers that for me is much heavier than any backpack I've carried. It's a necessary burden though, and a muscle I need to strengthen if I want to get better at it. Everyone's a stranger when you first meet them, so the only way to ever get close to anyone is to be willing to be vulnerable and exposed at some point. I was unwilling that day. Though I could practice my vulnerability in a different way, with a literal kind of exposure...so I stayed in my room and sent naked snapchats to my husband. I believe it was a good compromise.

After a wonderful night's sleep in what felt like the most comfortable bed ever made, I was ready to face the strangers at the breakfast table. The strain of being cordial must have been even more than anticipated because for the life of me I cannot remember one thing about our conversation. Though there was one specific thing I needed to discuss with Jess - how many mile chips could she help me cash in?

CASHING IN

Just three miles. Jess knew of a place she could drive me that would save me three miles of the trail, and she added it was a shame that my skipped miles would have been easy ones. No matter, better than a stick in the eye, as my mom used to say. So including the one mile I avoided when Papa Joe picked me up, only four cheater chips would be gone. I was really hoping to improve my odds of not having to use an Uber and cash in all six at once, but maybe I would find a good way to skip miles later and be glad for my extra fake chips to help me with my justification. (If you think that is foreshadowing, you would be correct.)

Pulling the car over at the spot I would get back on the trail, Jess had some last words of advice: "I don't know what it is about this upcoming hill, but I've had several experienced hikers end up back at my house because they got turned around at the top and called me when they found themselves back down on this road. There must be some confusing blazes, so just be aware." After acknowledging that without her warning that is exactly something I would do, (and thinking it was just the kind of punishment karma would dole out for my cheater ways) I thanked her and was back at it. My 16 hours of rest were over.

No karmic reckoning; Jess never received another call from me, though another night there would have felt more like a reward than a punishment. My actual punishment was spending a lot of time being extremely paranoid, worrying I had somehow gotten turned around, and then cursing myself for being too cheap to have bought more Guthook's maps when I had service. As soon as I came to a road and saw that another hiker was using their phone, I took advantage of the bars and downloaded more maps. The rules I gave myself for how many times it could be checked were broken before nightfall, but I did try.

Waiting for the transaction to finish, I thought flexing some of my sociable muscles and at least asking the other hiker's name was a good idea. When she replied "Close Call," I had a good excuse to continue trying to make more conversation. After reminding her of our meeting/not actual meeting, I told her how surprised I was to catch up to her with my slower than average pace.

"I'm really struggling with motivation. I left the trail a while back for a few days to see family, and now that I'm back, I just don't have the drive I did. I do want to complete the trail, but every day I care a little less if I actually finish. I'm wasting far too much time on my phone lately because I miss everybody," she explained.

Damn phones. I put mine away and swore to leave it, then wished her well as I left. Because this was a Sunday, there were more day hikers on the trail than usual, and after a few hours, I ran into a couple who seemed extra interested in wanting to talk to thru-hikers. Explaining my "500/50/5" theme always made me feel slightly better about disappointing folks with the news I was not a thru-hiker, and they were kind enough to act slightly impressed with my ambitions. But they were more concerned about the thru-hiker they had just met.

"There's a gal called Close Call who seemed so discouraged. If you catch up with her, please give her some encouragement," they pleaded with me with a degree of seriousness that would have been used if it was their own daughter. Of course, Close Call had whisked by me mere minutes after I left her, and still had time to have a pow-wow with these folks without fear of even getting in my sights. Not to imply I was annoyed; I was too struck by the intensity of concern these people had for a complete stranger.

There are times when I let the depravity of mankind steal my hope - especially after watching Dateline. But how can you not see the beauty of humanity when you run across random love like this? All I could do was smile, and promise to do my best if I saw her again. It saddens me to say I lied. Not intentionally, but the fact is that though I did see her again several times, I was 100% unhelpful. I cannot tell you why I didn't attempt to engage with her more, except to say I just didn't have the genuine concern for her that they did. My own humanity is something I can embrace and love more than ever before, but that doesn't mean I can't see clearly that I am still a part of the very egoism I hate. Grace to me means the ability to forgive myself, along with everyone else, for struggling to live as if my neighbor is another me - worthy of the exact same love and care. Very few of us are free enough to be able to love everyone that well, though it did seem that this sweet couple was doing a pretty good job at it. I'll keep hoping to get there because forgiving myself doesn't mean I lack the desire to be better.

Pack Rat caught me within a mile of his goal for the day. He was having the "shouldn't the shelter be here already?" frustration that was my daily existence, so I tried to help take his mind off it as we walked and talked together for a while. When the sign finally appeared for the South Wilcox Shelter, I could tell he was hoping I'd quit early so he could have some company. I was tempted, but quitting early would have felt like a waste of my cheater chips. Nope, I absolutely had to get in another two miles to the next shelter. Stopping now would only mean adding two miles to the upcoming day's already too far 14 miles to Upper Goose Cabin.

After leaving Pack Rat, it was all I could do to stay away from my Guthook's app. After hiking what felt like another five miles, I finally caved. It's crazy how much I would psych myself up for what it would reveal.

"Don't you dare freak out if it says you have a mile left. I'm only letting you check to be sure you didn't miss it, and I swear, you will not be checking again."

Thank God I didn't have to keep arguing with myself because I had less than a half mile to go. But then there is the trail off the trail that you have to take to get to the shelter. If these were any longer than a couple tenths of a mile, I would get exceptionally annoyed. And of course, this one was .04 away.

A tenth of a mile used to be something I didn't think much about. It really wasn't even something to consider at all - simply a fraction used to round up or down to an actual mile. The AT changed this for me. Did you know there are 528 feet in a tenth of a mile? I didn't either; I just googled it. But I was aware that 300 of my steps equal roughly that because I would often have to count just to keep my feet moving. If only I could have widened my gait like Mr. Know-it-all Slim Jim suggested, life would have been easier. Anyway, 1200 more steps off-trail to the North Mount Wilcox Shelter, and day 18 was in the books.

Quite a bit of commotion came from the shelter that night, but I was just fine missing the party and staying put in my tent. Unlike my experience at RPH where my need for companionship was awakened, my time at Ms. Treat's made me feel socially fatigued. Reclusive Kellbell was back in top form. It took some will in the morning to force myself to walk toward the shelter to say hello to whoever was there. Although my inner hermit was feeling strong, my desire to be at least slightly friendly got the upper hand.

"Kellbell! I was wondering if that tent out back was you!"

Lightning Rod was in his element; surrounded by people, joking and telling stories. He had an energy that drew everyone and made him the center of attention, so it always felt like the fact he knew me upgraded my status a little.

He caught me up with his tale of staying in Sheffield; a horrible hotel with cigarette burns in the mattress at a ridiculous cost of $170 a night, with an insult to injury extra mistaken charge for two nights. Somehow he managed to make this all sound exciting - just another part of his grand adventure. Nevermind if it's a stay in a mansion or a skanky hotel room, the joy is in the journey. Everything a puppy does is new and fun and celebrated with enthusiasm. I really should have tried to make friends with grumpy cat Debbie, because I think we had more in common.

Even though LR gave me a slight in with the others, I still couldn't help feeling misplaced and uncomfortable. With the excuse of no time to shoot the breeze, I excused myself and started in on the 14 mile day.

If I thought the .04 of a mile to the last shelter was bad, the full half mile to Upper Goose Cabin felt 10 times worse. Not able to concentrate enough to count my steps anymore, and too tired to want to fight with myself about looking at Guthook's, I plodded forward like a complete zombie...only slower. Imagine a zombie who had lost even the passion to eat people; that was my state.

"Hey, you almost won today Kellbell! So close. But the hare has it this time," LR playfully taunted as he whizzed by. He was lucky I wasn't an actual zombie, because it almost gave me enough motivation to try to catch him.

TOO POOPED TO PARTY

The Upper Goose Cabin is a shelter anomaly. I knew it was a "cabin," but that could mean any number of things. The fact it is owned by the National Park Service and is for the exclusive use of AT hikers had me envisioning something similar to Ralph's Peak Cabin - basically a shelter with more walls and some extra space for beds. What I found was something else entirely.

When I came upon it, my relief to be done hiking for the day could not even be processed, because the sensation of being overwhelmed by people was so overpowering. It's a strange feeling, going from hiking alone for over 10 hours with nothing but the trees around you, to suddenly popping in on such a huge hippie party scene.

Hikers were everywhere. Clothes were hanging everywhere. The cabin was painted bright red, and a full two stories high. The front porch had a staircase going up to the second story balcony, and every inch of it was draped in Patagonia and North Face sportswear. All of it felt a little like an assault to the senses.

With prayers under my breath for enough space for me to stay, I searched for the caretaker amidst the dreadlocks and tattoos. It didn't take long, because he stuck out like a sore thumb with his tucked-in collared shirt and gray hair; and yes, he said there was room at the inn. When he asked me if I wanted a bunk upstairs or a tent site out back, I froze like a deer in headlights. My bunk sleeping reputation thus far was at best unfavorable; however, the thought of walking even another 10 feet to set up a tent had me declaring "bed please" before I could analyze the pros and cons another minute.

Even going up the stairs to claim my bed was a struggle, I wanted to entirely stop moving so badly. If it wasn't for my need to eat, I may have just laid down right there and died to the world. I managed to make it back down to the picnic tables with the others, but then could not focus on what my body should be doing.

"Water, I need water, but where's my filter? Shit, it's upstairs with my pack. Do I even need one? But I do need my stove. God, look how far away the bathroom is. Do you think anyone would notice if I went behind that tree? Oh wait, there's Pack Rat. I really should say hi. Should I get my water first? No, I really have to pee. Can I lay down and die first?"

Functionally brain dead, I knew I was officially now a hazard. As close to a literal zombie as humanly possible, I was frightened to try and operate my stove - especially with everyone around and a roof over the table that could theoretically catch on fire. Desperate for a warm meal and already loathing granola bars, I went ahead and took my chances.

Pack Rat sat next to me and we cooked together while watching the chaos of the youngsters buzzing about like a swarm of hyperactive bohemians. I really wanted to interact more; I wanted to be funny and engaging and have them like me and feel like I belonged...but the best I could do was to not fall asleep in my bowl of top ramen.

Watching the show was very entertaining though. There was a good fire going, and somehow someone had brought a whole bunch of hot dogs, so it became like a big barbeque. Stories started coming up about hitching, something almost everyone does to get into a town quickly to resupply. They were talking about a hiker named Freight Train, and how of course he'll be back quick because he always gets picked up easily.

"If I'm with him, a car stops in like five minutes," a scrawny guy named Tarzan started in. "But if I'm alone, they don't even slow down!"

"Well, have you looked in a mirror lately?" someone called out, and the crowd roared. He did look a real mess, even by hiking standards. Laughing along with them, he nodded his head, obviously well aware of his dismal state. Tarzan was a perfect name, he was so clearly a wild child. But don't picture the muscular movie Tarzan, not at all. He was like a Disney Tarzan/Mowgli crossbreed. Except even skinnier.

He got onto another story, about some kids teasing him. Why they were harassing him I can't recall, but it must have been when he was trying to get a ride. He described how he reached into his pocket for a rock and threw it at them.

"You carry rocks in your pockets?! Why in the world would you do that?" another hiker shouted out in bewilderment. You could tell Tarzan was taken aback for a second as if it never occurred to him to question why he did such a thing.

"Well, to throw them at kids. Duh." Again, the crowd erupted in laughter. Then the laughter morphed into cheers as another hiker suddenly appeared literally out from the bushes.

"Freight Train!! Wow, that was so fast!!" everyone praised as he came up to the picnic table and plunked down a couple buckets of fried chicken. I thought that my mental state had evolved into actual hallucinations, so I had to ask what was going on. Freight Train explained that he left the group earlier because he had heard a road nearby and thought he would go get more food for everyone. So he bushwhacked until he found it, hitched to the closest town, and brought back the chicken because "he had some extra energy." I looked at him as if he was an alien. Extra energy while you are hiking the AT? He must have been the Jack Russel version of a puppy. All I could do was shake my head and take my old dog body to bed at the ripe old hour of 8:00 pm.

Earplugs made it possible to sleep because the party went on all night. I didn't mind being in the middle of all the activity - the bigger "con" I wish I would have considered with the upstairs bunk option was the bathroom situation. With a tent, peeing is just a few steps away. Now I was facing a trip down the stairs and out to the privy which felt like a mile away. All the other shelters had signs saying it was good to pee in the forest; it saved room in the outhouse hole for the more important #2. But here at Upper Goose Cabin, they had special outhouses with a poop hole AND a separate hole for pee. Considering the amount of folks who were there, I guess I can understand why. I peed in the bushes a couple of feet from the house anyway, and I'm not going to apologize. What I am ashamed about is what happened after breakfast.

I had heard rumors floating around that the caretaker makes pancakes for everyone, but it seemed too good to be true. It wasn't. The morning excitement at the table crammed with hikers was palpable. Of course, it was not even a fraction of all who were there; most of the kids were still sleeping. Many may have still been down by the lake where the skinny dipping and major partying commenced throughout the evening. Hearing some of the whisperings around me of the goings-on reminded me again of why I'm grateful to be too old for that shit.

As we sat and waited for the pancakes, I tried my best to make conversation. My zombie status had been downgraded to a level five, so I felt somewhat capable of merriment; though most of my joke attempts were crashing and burning. The fretful feeling of being an awkward outsider started descending upon me. When the ginormous stack of pancakes was plopped in front of me, panic set in.

"Don't you dare pick at that like you do all your food. They are all going to notice, and you will look like an idiot! A real hiker would scarf this down and ask for more. EAT EVERY LAST BITE YOU LOSER!!!"...if you haven't already noticed, my critical voice isn't very nice.

I gave it my very best effort, honestly.

"You call that an effort? If I knew you were going to fail that bad, I would have made you give some of your pancakes to someone else, even with your huge paranoia of getting laughed at. But now it's too late because you've created a big mound of mush nobody wants. What are you going to do now? Put it in the garbage disposal? Good luck with that dipshit, because there isn't even a sink here." Yep. She can be a real bitch.

I tried to ask all lackadaisical like what we were supposed to do with our dishes...while still eating of course, so as not to bring any suspicion about my intentions. Waiting until I thought the others were distracted enough to not notice that I was decidedly not part of the clean plate club, I bolted outside. With my soggy leftovers in hand, I rushed to the washing station where I had been told everyone was supposed to take care of their own plate.

Frantically scanning the area, no food dump bucket was to be found. Is there never even a scrap of food that isn't consumed here? REALLY?

Knowing I could not bring myself to ask where to put my pathetically uneaten and horribly wasted heap of flapjack slush, I instead choose to wash my plate with everything still on it, allowing the doughy mess to mix in with all the sudsy water. A quick rinse in the next bin, dry, stack, and I was out of there.

"Who the hell just washed their dish with all their disgusting food still on it?" came the bellowed inquest from another hiker just minutes later. I looked around like, "Yeah, who would dare perform such a vile act?"...all the while fighting the urge to hide under a table.

"Aren't you too old to be feeling like a five year who just got scolded by the babysitter?"

Yes inner voice, I am. Can you please shut up now? We gotta get going before anyone asks any more questions.

TRAIL SURRENDER

I recall almost nothing about August 21st. The only reason I can write anything about it at all is because of my phone. A YouTube channel was the easiest way for friends and family to check in on me, so I created one before I left to download videos on. Looking back at it now, I can see that on August 21st I spent a solid three minutes bitching about the AT. My struggles with the steep hills, slippery rocks, constant tree cover, and overall lack of substantial recovery time had helped to morph my general dislike into actual contempt. The AT had become offensive to me.

There were times I'd fantasize about meeting the creator of the trail. I'd curse him out, kick over his garbage can, TP his house - any unpleasant action that would channel my mean spirit as I huffed and puffed up another stupid hill. Of course, I knew there was no such man. The three men who chaired the Appalachian Trail Conference at various stages during the 16 years before it became an actuality are all long gone. In fact, so is the trail that they helped construct, because 99% of it has been rebuilt or relocated since its completion in 1937. Though of course none of this matters when you just want to blame and hate someone for the misery you are enduring.

As soon as the trail would level out, so would my grumbling. Then shame would set in. Why was I letting these climbs get to me so much? It's true that Washington had spoiled me. We develop a sort of view addiction there. Hiking efforts should result in a jaw-dropping scene; that is the expectation because it almost always does. Washingtonians are view snobs - we can't help it. So hiking my ass off only to be rewarded with an immediate horrific decline on rocks or mud would always cause my overindulged West Coast sensibilities to protest, "no fair!"

The good news is, the AT taught me to look for other things to appreciate about nature besides the mountain top experience. The adorable little frogs who were always hopping across the trail, the brilliant orange salamanders that I at first thought were plastic toys, the mushrooms in every shape and size imaginable - they all developed a deeper sense of wonder in me. They became companions in a way...well, except for the mushrooms. I knew better than to befriend them too much.

August 21st ended at a stealth site close to a stream. Due to my overall blackout for this day, I only know this because of the daily notes I also documented on my phone.

"8:30 start. 5:30 end. Stealth site by brook."

Apparently some days I didn't feel like writing much. I have a faint recollection of stopping earlier than I intended, though statistically speaking, that would be a good bet.

"Woke to rain. Naked camper."

Looks like August 22nd started off with a bang. I actually remember this day quite well. After hiking the first few miles in the rain, I stumbled upon another stealth site, complete with a bare ass man. He looked to be just going about his morning; like wearing clothes before 10:00 am was not part of his routine. He did try to quickly cover himself when he saw me, and then I had a dilemma. Is it better to say hi, even though then he'll know I saw his junk? Or do I act so focused on the trail that I didn't notice him, even if it makes me seem unfriendly? He was far enough in the woods that pretending not to see him felt plausible (even if highly unlikely) so I went on by without so much as a "nice butt."

The rain went from bad to worse...like standing in the shower kind of bad. I've never seen so much mud. This was concerning because supposedly I wasn't even to the muddiest section of the AT - what everyone referred to as "Vermud." For many of the days in Massachusetts, it felt near impossible to keep forward momentum, because so much time was being wasted looking for rocks to hop across, or any other way to navigate around the seemingly endless La Brea tar pit obstacles. My guidebook instructions for Vermont were to "stay on trail; do not attempt to go around mud," so I was pretty sure I was going to be a very naughty hiker in that state. It seemed at this point that "not going around" mud that was any worse than Massachusetts' could only result in a mammoth type of catastrophe. (Yes, pun intended if you caught it.)

After a very slow nine miles, my ambitions were telling me there was no other option but to keep pushing ahead and catch up on miles; but my guidebook was telling me otherwise in the form of an upcoming town. Practically sliding down the mountain and covered in muck, all I could think about was Dalton's cheapest motel, the Shamrock Inn.

The AT goes right through the town of Dalton; it was strange walking through a neighborhood and having folks sitting on their porch and waving to me as I went by. When I saw a liquor shop named "Kelly's" directly in front of the inn, I took it as a sign in more ways than one. I surrendered, and went ahead and paid too much for the Shamrock's next to last room.

With wine in hand from the prophetic store, I saw that a group of hikers were also staying at the inn. The sun had, at last, peaked out, and they were congregated around an outdoor table near the entrance. The thought entered my mind to go over and try to make friends; the kumbaya experience I was hoping for was not going to happen without some effort on my part, after all. But instead, I avoided even making eye contact and disappeared into my room. I swear it wasn't because I didn't want to share my booze, though it's true drinking the whole bottle by myself was not a problem. It's just that being alone was fine by me; introverts even like it. Is that bad? Maybe...but at that time and place, I gave myself permission to crawl into my shell with my cheap merlot and be what I was with no judgment. There are days to push yourself, and there are days to give yourself a break. When you can embrace that for a minute, it's a real relief.

Even though the Shamrock Inn was just what the doctor ordered, I couldn't help feeling a little guilty. In only three more days I'd be at another hotel, though that stay was not optional. My food supply was already shipped and waiting for me at the Catamount Motel, since I expected to already be there. Reworking mile configurations in the room that night, I figured the next three days of 14, 11, and 15 miles were reasonable goals. Of course, I winced even thinking about the 15, but quickly bolstered my resolve with reminders of how much it would all be worth it. If I could stay on task for the next three days, I would be half way done, and only a day behind my master plan.

Maybe it was the wine, maybe a case of ignoring facts when you want something to be true, but my calculations were flawed. I was in for a surprise come day three, I just didn't know it yet.

Blissfully ignorant of what lay ahead and somehow able to rally myself out of bed early, I said goodbye to the Shamrock feeling refreshed and confident. Much of the day was town walking - so much better than sloshing through mud. As I strolled through Cheshire, I fervently tried to convince myself not to hunt down a restaurant. Enough spoiling had gone on in Dalton; plus I needed to keep the pedal to the metal. But darn it if there wasn't the cutest little ice cream place right on the trail.

Because I was allowing myself yet another break, I decided I had to push myself in a different way. It was time I tried being social again, so I took my cone toward the group of hikers sitting outside of Diane's Twist Shop. As I reluctantly walked to the crowded picnic tables, I recognized Tarzan from the Upper Goose Cabin and plopped down right next to him. Breaking the ice, I asked him where he had stayed the night. Oh boy, he had quite the tale to tell.

Having had too much to drink, and deciding to hike at night, he had the misfortune of his headlamp going out, which resulted in a fall. Even though now bloody and without light, he still continued on, trying to make it to Cheshire. Coyotes caught his sent and started circling him, thinking he was a wounded deer. (Not a conclusion I would have made, but okay.) He could only keep them at bay by belting them with rocks, (remember he always carried some in his pockets to throw at kids...who would have guessed this was unforeseen brilliance) and finally stumbled into Cheshire as the coyotes gradually gave up the chase. Certainly, he would have become a meal if it wasn't for the town, and the nice ice cream lady letting him sleep in this very yard.

"That would have been the worst meal those coyotes ever had," I teased before I could think to edit myself. That kind of humor is best left until you know someone, but sometimes I can't help myself.

"Ain't that the truth!" Tarzan roared. Then everyone laughed, thank God. It was the first big laugh I'd gotten, and it felt good.

When I reached the shelter that night, there was already a large group there, but for the first time, many of them recognized me. Even if they called me Cowbell, it still felt like I was starting to fit in just a little. I was even invited to come with them to the top of the mountain where there was to be some sort of big party. I remembered hearing talk of this in town. Half of them were staying in Cheshire to do errands, then they would take an Uber to the Mount Greylock Summit Tower to stealth camp on the grounds. This other half taking a break at the shelter were obviously hiking to meet up with the Uber group. "Just another three miles to the top," they said, "you should come with us!"

Of course, I only chuckled at the offer. Even if I did have the energy, I didn't have the party spirit. I had gotten my one laugh for the day; best to quit the social game while I was ahead.

A very nice group camping spot was behind the shelter, so I claimed it and prayed an actual group didn't come in and scold me. Two other solo hikers trickled in, and seeing that I had already broken the rules, went ahead and joined me. We all sat at the picnic table that night and ate our dinners together like it was our own little family meal. For the first time, there was no tension and effort in making conversation; I might even say it was relaxing.

"The trail always provides." This is something a hiker affirmed after recounting his story of getting medical care for a crushed leg from a fellow hiker who just happened to be at the right place at the right time. My need for companionship pales in comparison, I know...but the trail was merciful regardless.

Some may feel uncomfortable talking about the trail in such a way; as if it's some omnipotent deity. I do not, because for me "the trail" is just another way of saying "the Spirit." I could go deep here - I have almost 10 years of deconstructed religious ideas under my belt just begging to be unleashed. I'll restrain myself for now, except to say I do believe the Spirit provides, and she moves in mysterious ways. The gentleness in which I'm encouraged to open up, forgive myself, be in the moment, and surrender to love all confirm this to me. Maybe the Spirit of God is in and around us all the time, and even our protective shells can't fend it off forever.

LESSONS IN NON-ASSHOLENESS

At breakfast, I realized the man sitting next to me was the "naked hiker" from day 21. No, he wasn't going about his morning routine unclothed, though that would have been far more interesting. He was recalling his last couple of days, and it clicked when he described his camp spot.

"You're the guy with the nice butt!"

He might have laughed if I actually said it, but I didn't want to chance it. He seemed like the type to think it was funny, but coming across like a creepy old lady felt like too big a risk. Leave it to me to ruin my best AT encounter thus far by taking it too far with a joke. Best to play it safe so I could leave my one night family with the tidbit of social confidence they had given me.

Heading up to the summit of Mount Greylock, I had a single priority...find a hamburger. Confusing signs and road crossings, throngs of tourists buzzing about, the 92 foot tall shining scepter tower beckoning me to its wonders - everything tried, but could not distract me from my laser-focused goal.

The highest peak in Massachusetts, Mount Greylock has a lot to offer, and it was bustling. Being surrounded by so many people while I was in hiker mode always seemed to make my brain a little fuzzy, but I knew the Bascom Lodge was where I needed to be. When the huge building came into view, I was really surprised the only thing my guidebook mentioned about this place was that you could buy lunch. Considering the name and the size, you would think there would be lodging offered, but that did not seem to be the case. I tried to keep focused on beelining it to the restaurant, but my thoughts did wander briefly to considering where the hiker party took place the previous night. As I was wondering how anyone could possibly be stealthy in such a public area, my mind suddenly cleared of all thoughts when I caught the scent of sizzling meat.

After staring at the menu for far too long, I ordered at the counter, then looked around to where I should sit. Even with a shower less than 48 hours behind me, my aroma was not compatible with a contained area. Deciding it was worth the chance someone could steal it, I went ahead and left my phone inside to charge and chose a table outside.

"No good deed goes unpunished you know," my inner skeptic warned, but I'm glad I didn't listen. My phone was fine, and it was good to believe the trail was not turning me into a complete asshole. Thankfully considering others before myself from time to time was still within my ability.

Another hiker sat down to join me, and I was pleased to discover my heart did not fill with dread. "Evermore" was from Germany, and though I can't say our conversation was without clumsy moments, it was still rather pleasant. Getting another morsel of confidence in my abilities to be somewhat charming was a good reward, and I savored it. Not quite as tasty as the food though, which I did manage to nearly fully consume.

After exchanging a few stories, Evermore opened up about a hiking fail. He confessed that somehow he got turned around at the top of a recent mountain. He considered himself above that kind of mistake; how can not realizing you are going back the way you came even be possible for someone who has spent so many weeks doing nothing but hiking? I was glad to be able to assure him he wasn't alone, and how if it were not for the help of my homestay host, I'd be most likely telling the same story.

It was so easy getting caught up in the novelty of sitting at a table and eating and chatting like a halfway civilized human, I ended up lingering longer than I should have. I didn't realize this until I was four miles away from camp, with only a couple hours of daylight left. What was I thinking lounging around like that? Knowing I had to make it to Pete's Spring Campsite, the panic of possibly setting up my tent in the dark started setting in. The numerous signs warning me of the forbidden-ness of setting camp wherever you pleased made it clear that quitting early was not an option if I wanted to keep up on my non-assholeness. The immediate rush of anxiety I get when I think about hiking in the dark caused me to travel much faster than what is advisable on a steep downhill of roots and mud.

The fall I took was jarring, but I was lucky. The mud was my friend this day, making a soft landing for both knees, even though I hit hard. Pack Rat was not so fortunate...but that story comes later. Though he would bring to mind this moment, and how any tumble could bring my AT adventure to a quick end.

Just as the last hill climb of the day was starting to ramp up in difficulty, I spotted the party crew down below, setting up right next to the stream that all the signs explicitly warned not to camp next to.

"Assholes."

The thought made me laugh at myself. Self-righteous smugness can come as easy as tripping over a rock, so I at least allow myself to have a sense of humor about it. We all know I'd be right down there with them if I knew I could get away with it, so I pushed my jealous hopes they'd get caught aside, and instead wished them well in my heart.

"Hey, Kellbell!"

The greeting out of nowhere startled me out of my thoughts. A glance backward revealed the source - Freight Train coming towards me full steam ahead.

As silly as it seems, I actually imagined he was sent up by the gang to entice me to come join them. My brain did a few circles as he approached - feeling flattered, feeling worried, feeling conflicted. Obviously, I couldn't accept their offer if I was going to obey the rules, which I was really trying to be better at. But I also wanted to be better at opening up and interacting more, and lately, I was kind of on a streak. Maybe this was exactly the right challenge at the right time to get me completely out of my shell.

All these mental gymnastics were completely in vain because Freight Train was just doing what Freight Train does - expelling energy. The Vermont border was only a few miles ahead, so he wanted to cross it, just for fun; then turn back around to camp with everyone else. Let me remind you, this was late in the day, probably around 6:00 pm. He had hiked from the Mount Greylock party I had missed. I bet he hardly slept. Yet, he decided he just couldn't be done and enjoy sitting around camp; he needed to go across the border, for no apparent reason at all except for his abnormal desire to keep moving. He, of course, had left his pack back at camp, so I suggested he should carry mine since he was feeling so energetic. He laughed and said he really should, then zipped off like the alien hybrid I was further convinced he actually was.

Watching him bound away, I immediately felt regret for making it sound like a joke. Why didn't I offer him money? I seriously would have given him a twenty to just drop my pack off for me, and I sulked the rest of the way to Pete's Spring thinking about it.

I barely made it before dark. It was a lonely place, not a soul around, and it had a creepy feel that made me think about bears. Most likely it was the dusk bringing on its usual paranoia, but I was afraid to even cook. I couldn't even look forward to seeing Freight Train coming back from his pointless endeavor, because like usual, this camp was several tenths of a mile off-trail. Cocooned in my sleeping bag, ears wide open, chewing my

God awful protein bar, I thought it best to get out my guide book and go over my upcoming day as a distraction.

And there it was, in black and white. I didn't have a cringe worthy 15 miles to my road pick up. I had a horrific 17.8.

At least it worked - bears were completely off my mind. The only thoughts now were of the Cantmount room that was already paid for, and the fact that wasting that money was not even in my realm of possibility. Those miles would get done, period. I had until 7:00 pm sharp because the motel proprietor had made it clear that was the last pick up of the day. The clear instructions were: call for your ride when you reach the top of Harmon Hill because that is the only place there is reception. Then you will have an hour to make it the two miles down to the road, where the shuttle will be waiting at the parking lot across the street. Do not, I repeat, do not think you can call once you reach the road. Zero coverage, with any carrier. No calling a cab, an Uber, a friend - if you miss the shuttle, you will be hitchhiking.

I'm kind of impressed I didn't cry that night. My alarm was set for 5:30 am, and I somehow fell asleep with the belief that all would be well. Whatever hell the next day brought, a bed and shower was in my immediate future.

CHILL OUT ALREADY

After making the call on Harmon Hill at 5:30 pm, you would think I'd be relieved. My alarm had gone off on time, I hiked faster than I had ever hiked in my life, I was a half hour ahead of schedule, my phone still had charge and the call went through fine. My ride was on its way - everything had gone pretty much perfectly. Maybe too perfect.

I don't know about you, but I get suspicious when things go so well. There's gotta be a catch. Everything is going to fall apart any second because that's just how life is. Best to brace yourself...tense all up for when the big disappointing blow comes, and it won't hurt so bad.

This is another thing I'm trying to do differently in life. Maybe just enjoy that things are good for a moment? Maybe stop thinking about how it's going to be horrible any minute now? And so what if it might be horrible? You've gotten through everything horrible so far.

But this day I was not doing so well with this new way of thinking.

"I am going to kill myself trying to get down this freakishly steep hill. Stupid thru-hikers who can cruise two miles an hour no problem. Why didn't I tell them I wasn't a thru-hiker?! I could have just asked to get picked up at the cutoff hour of 7:00 pm, but no, that would have required admitting being that slow. Pride...stupid, stupid pride. Well, I'm not going to make it, and the driver is going to leave, that's all. I'll have to hitchhike, and I'll probably get picked up by a serial killer. The end. Unless I die falling down this abhorrent hill first."

It's not that I truly believed these things. It's my way of "bracing" - imagining the worst so that anything less than the worst won't feel so bad. It's a bad habit, and not helpful. All that worry and grumbling, and for what? A waste of emotional energy, that's it.

When I got to the parking lot, I actually had to wait for my ride because I was a couple minutes early. But of course, the worrying didn't stop. "What if they don't see me, what if they aren't coming, what if..."

Then an old sedan with a grizzled looking driver pulled up and he declared out the window, "You must be the one I'm here to pick up."

Still not relieved. Still quite worried. I was imagining some kind of official looking van with "Catamount Motel" painted on the side. How do I know this isn't some predator who knows hikers get picked up here? Maybe he just happened to time it right, and I'm the sucker who is going to fall for it.

"For heaven's sake, just shut up already and get in the damn car."

That's my inner voice again, in case you couldn't tell. Yep, I was completely done with my paranoid self, once again. Being aware of danger is one thing, and you should always listen if your sixth sense is giving you a heads up. But in this instance, I knew I was stuck on the tragic ending mentality, and at that moment I gave myself permission to let it go. Just embrace the fact that I had actually made it.

The switch from paranoid to jovial was instantaneous. I was practically woozy with glee. That poor driver - I rambled on like a drunk the entire way. Finally letting the relief flow, it was like a flood. I gushed on about how worried I was that I wasn't going to make it; that I would miss the shuttle and have to camp in the parking lot.

"Oh, you shouldn't have worried! I would have waited for you. I only tell the boss I won't do any pick-ups after seven o'clock because that's my happy hour," he divulged.

Now if that isn't a lesson to chill out about life, I don't know what is. I told him I was ready for happy hour too. Where the hell is happy hour?

"Oh, I just go to the convenience store across the street. They sell beer and wine."

Before feeling disappointed there was no actual happy hour, I asked myself if I really thought for one second I had the energy to hit the town. That was a big fat no. But as we drove through the main street of Bennington, I started to reconsider. Not only did I just set a personal record for most miles in a day, but tomorrow would also be my "I'm half way done!" day of 25. Bennington was cute and looked like a place I could find lots of happy hours to commemorate this occasion and a lot of other hikers to celebrate with too. But as high on life as I felt while sitting in the car, the second we arrived and I had to actually move, I understood there would be no walking to town. I was going to be lucky to make it to the convenience store to partake in the Catamount way of doing happy hour.

Being so ecstatic about getting to the motel without disaster, I had failed to realize my true state...100% zombie. SO gone. The manager explained their laundry service, take out food options, the short walk into town to the many nice restaurants, but I just stared. I gave him my credit card and then forgot it. I lost my key. I left my backpack at the desk. I kept wandering back and forth from the lobby to my room like a dementia patient.

"Hey, the staff is having barbecue tonight, and we have way more than we can eat. Can I bring a plate of food to your room?" the kind man at the desk asked me after I toddled into the foyer for the third time. He was probably wondering if he was going to need to feed me too.

In the morning I took a look around my room. Total disarray. Besides having my own happy hour and sending lots of snaps to my husband, I had done little else. My plate of barbecue wasn't even finished. Clothes unwashed, new food supplies unpacked, everything everywhere...and I needed to get a move on if I was going to get my planned 11 miles in and not squander the one day I had worked so hard to get caught up on.

I'm going to let you in on a little secret. Before writing this book and looking more closely at my original plan, I didn't know I had gotten a whole three days off; I believed it to be only two. In Bennington, I was happy to have made up one of my two lost days, but the truth was I had made up two of my lost three days! If I had known this, it may have been easier to give myself permission to lay off the gas a little.

As it stood though, thinking about the effort it took to make up just one day, and considering I still had another to go, made not getting in my required miles seem reckless. I only sat in bed staring at my stuff all the same.

After a tearful call to my husband who encouraged me it was okay, I gave in and allowed myself a pass. No, not an extra day at the hotel, but a greatly lessened goal of only two miles to the next shelter.

It had been so many years since I had an in-depth conversation with Ken over the phone. We would talk for hours when we dated; but once you are married, phone conversations are no longer necessary. Each year you become more familiar with each other, and each year you take each other a little more for granted. I don't think that is entirely a bad thing. You know each other. You've heard each other's stories, you understand each other's thinking, you've learned how the other person ticks...and in that knowing there is comfort. You don't have to try so hard. Yes, there can be a bad side to that, but there is also the lovely security in knowing you are safe with that person.

And then you get those pockets in life when you get to realize just how grateful you are to have someone who knows all your crap and is still there anyway. That phone call was one of those moments.

"Absence makes the heart grow fonder," they say. I have to admit, I wasn't 100% sure it would be true for Ken and I. In our 30 plus years together we have become very separate people. We've given each other license to be different from each other...different passions, different world views, different ways of handling emotions and life. The way we allow each other a high level of independence is something I appreciate, though it can lend itself to a false ideology of autonomy. There is a fine line between wanting to be self-sufficient, and not wanting to be vulnerable. I feared this 45 day separation would intensify these negative aspects of self-reliance to a degree where our feelings of connection would be lost.

Thankfully, the opposite was true. A greater connection was formed in the awareness of our need for each other. Not a needy, clingy need, but a longing and appreciative need. We are a part of each other, and it's a good thing.

Though, all this gratitude and bonding did not make getting back on the trail any easier. I stayed in my room for as long as was allowed - until the cleaning lady came knocking. A two mile day was little comfort, especially knowing this only meant more hours would be spent just laying in my tent. If only I could do a few more miles; but the shelter spacing did not allow for it. Though, maybe I could hope that somehow the trail would provide an alternative, just as it had been providing for everything I really needed thus far.

ALTERED OUTCOMES

I spotted Lightning Rod and his posse catching a ride into town when Happy Hour Jim dropped me back off at the trail in the large parking lot he had picked me up at the day before. My mood was immediately brightened...the tortoise was still in the lead! I only wished I could have rubbed it in a little, but they were pulling out by the time I got out of the car.

The trail became an immediate steep incline. I should have been happy that I only had two miles, but I wasn't. As of yet, I hadn't had a day where I stopped before I felt extremely ready to be done hiking, so quitting while I still had gas in my tank was not going to feel right at all. The thought persistently bothered me all morning.

It was only noonish when I reached the turnoff to the shelter. A good sized stream was crossing the trail there, and typically I would load up on water in case this was the only water source. I think I've already made it clear how much I hated having to walk any distance after arriving at camp to get my water. Typically, once I stopped moving, I wanted to keep as motionless as possible thereafter.

Once I took off my pack to get my water filter bags, I decided to make lunch instead. This should have made it obvious that I had no intention of stopping at this shelter, but at the time I told myself it was because it was a pretty spot. The truth is I was biding my time until I could be convinced to continue.

Before long a south bounder stopped to join me, and I told

him my predicament about wishing I could do more miles. He thought it was the dumbest thing he'd ever heard.

"I don't do miles," he informed me, "I do hours. I aim to start at 8:00 am and stop at 6:00 pm. If I feel like going further, great. If not, then I don't. It's that simple. You really should try it."

"Well, it may be that simple for you...you must be another asshole hiker who ignores signs saying you can't camp anywhere you feel like it. I'm an ex-asshole, so that makes things more complicated."

Unspoken thoughts again, but I only nodded and said it was an interesting idea. It did make me realize I hadn't seen any signs yet, and then I remembered I had crossed into Vermont the previous day. Restrictions must be much less in this state.

"Are there any good stealth spots between here and the next shelter?" I inquired. He assured me there was, but I still wasn't convinced I should go for it. The forecast was for thunderstorms soon. I should be smart and just stay put and keep dry. Then another guest came through - a local trail runner who stopped for a few moments to catch his breath.

"Great day, isn't it!" he cheerily announced. I'll never understand how runners are so chipper, but I did agree it was a pleasant enough day, then added it was too bad rain would be coming soon.

"It doesn't feel like rain. I can tell. Look at the clouds and the way they are moving. Nope, we're safe. No rain today."

Though I was pretty sure he wasn't a meteorologist, he was convincing enough that I was finally persuaded. The trail had given me the nudges I needed. A couple of extra miles may not seem that important, but I think they were crucial. Without them, it would have been 17 miles the following day to the Story Spring Shelter instead of 15, so I would have definitely stopped four miles sooner at the Kid Gore Shelter. (What a name right? Sounds like a place to slaughter children!) Skipping ahead a shelter set me up to have a very different agenda than had I not. It's easy to ponder how altogether changed my experience would have been had I not gone the extra two miles...maybe it could have even completely derailed everything.

A German movie made in 1998 explores this idea of how even seconds can utterly alter outcomes. "Run, Lola, Run" has three different endings, each resulting from whether Lola runs past, bumps into, or jumps over a man who is in her way. One concludes in glorious triumph, the other two with tragic fatality. The theater will always lend itself to the dramatic, so I doubt certain death was in my future had I not chosen to go a little further that day; but still, I can think myself into knots over that kind of stuff.

I didn't bring the amount of water I should have to the dry stealth spot that night. This trail made me extra lackadaisical about water, with its seemingly endless supply of streams. I continually pushed the envelope on how little I could carry, even though you really should always try to have more than you need, just in case. My lax attitude would bite me in the butt on more than one occasion, but thankfully never cost me more than some discomfort.

Because of the long lunch at the stream, which I had actually broken out my stove to cook a good meal, I opted to save the little water I had for a hot breakfast instead of making dinner. This gave me lots of time to lay in my sleeping bag and think about my plan for the upcoming week. I'm sure it took a long while to convince myself to aim for the 15 miles the following day. I probably told myself I could find a place to make camp if I wanted to quit early; I mean, the south bounder had made it sound so easy to just stop when you felt like it. The trail would provide, right?

The first shelter I came to the following day was a beauty, complete with its own porch. There were even some lovely flowering bushes surrounding it, and I saw my first hummingbirds zipping about in their mesmerizing fashion. Maybe I would have to get that tattoo I promised my daughter when I got home after all.

Before I left, I had a sentimental experience with a hummingbird, and after telling my 17 year old daughter about it, she suggested we both get hummingbird tattoos when I returned...mine to celebrate making my 50 day goal, hers to celebrate making it to 18, and both to pay tribute to my mom who died 18 years prior - two months shy of my daughter's birth. Why hummingbirds? That's a good question, and one I have a hard time answering.

I think about my mom a lot when I'm hiking alone; maybe just because there is so much time to think about everything. And then there are those times when it seems like I feel her. They don't come that often - very rarely, actually. A few times it has been when a little critter comes up close. Why it seems they are saying hello from my mom, I can't explain. But hummingbirds are my favorite, so even when I don't have that special feeling when I see them, they still always bring to mind my mom.

So it was surprising to me there had been no hummingbirds thus far on my journey, and I had even joked with my daughter over the phone that I thought my mom was trying to tell us she didn't like the tattoo idea. It was one of those "I'm kidding around, but actually a little serious too" kind of jokes, especially considering my mom was not a fan of body art. Seeing the tiny birds this day made me smile, and though I had no strong sense of my mother's presence, I did feel the tattoo idea was back on the table.

While considering these things and waiting for my macaroni and cheese to finish cooking, "Apple" showed up. I had passed him in the morning while he was breaking down his lonely camp. Unlike the naked hiker, he was fully clothed, so I had stopped to chat a little. He was obviously not in a good headspace, so I didn't stay long. Like Slim Jim and Close Call, he explained he had just returned to the AT after a short hiatus and was struggling. Trail breaks really did seem to screw everybody over.

He seemed in much better spirits as he joined me for lunch. It was nice to have company. I had to ask him about his name - I mean, Apple? He laughed and agreed it was a strange alias. Unfortunately, he had no big story to back it up, only that he eats them while hiking. When a fellow hiker took note with a "Hey Apple!" the name stuck. It made me glad I had taken Citizen's advice and named myself.

"At least it's one I can tell my mother," he laughed, "unlike some of the other considerations." Being that my friends had tried to name me "Fireball" back in Washington, I think I know what he meant.

When I first passed him, he had explained that his reason for leaving the trail for a few days was for a sad occasion, so I didn't want to bring it up for fear that someone had died. As we sat and ate, it was nice of him to clarify that it was his dog that had passed.

"I found out when I called my mom on top of Harmon Hill...dang, I'm surprised I didn't kill myself coming down that thing. I think I got to the road in a half hour, but I was really in a daze," he expounded. Picturing him flying down those rocks with tears in his eyes made my heart skip a beat, and I really wanted to put my hand on his shoulder. I could tell he didn't want to get emotional; so I just let it be, and we finished our lovely lunch date in comfortable silence.

The remainder of the day went smoothly, so I put away my phone to save my charge and relied solely on my guidebook. Reaching the described beaver pond, I would have gladly stopped for the day if I could have found anything flat and dry; but all was mushy, rocky, or bushy. Zero trail provision here. Oh well, my book said the shelter was just a mile past the beaver pond, so I was almost there. The "last mile blues" were even worse than usual, and it took all my resolve not to check Guthook's. At just about the time I was about to lose my shit, I came to what seemed to be the same beaver pond. Did I somehow just go in a circle?

Berating myself for thinking I could live without it, I dug my phone out in a panic. Then Guthook's clearly showed me that there were two very similar beaver ponds, one after the other. So I was obviously now at the one my guidebook was referring to...which meant I was only just starting my last mile. This is when I officially lost my shit.

Of course, this mile was straight up and rocky, and the daylight was fading. All this contributed to this being my worst mile yet. I was so pissed when I made it to the shelter that I didn't even feel relief, but had to try and act normal because a group of weekend campers was already there to greet me. Actually, they didn't greet me at all. It was obvious they were disappointed to have a grumpy section hiker show up and crash their party. I can't say I blame them. My attempts at acting friendly were forced and fakey, and so I hardly even tried. After getting my water and barely getting my tent up before dark, I skipped cooking dinner again and only ate a granola bar. Thinking about the new agenda I had created for the next few days made me lose my appetite anyway. I sent one text to Ken, then succumbed to my exhaustion:

"I'm feeling discouraged tonight. This week is going to be so hard. I just don't know if I have it in me. It doesn't seem to be getting any easier."

NOBODY SAID IT WAS EASY

We heard it from our parents, our teachers, our coaches, and even Coldplay. Of course, this wouldn't be easy...but I did expect it would get easier.

Hiking for me has never had anything to do with trying to get in a workout, and so I didn't worry too much about not being in shape for this trip. My previous backpacks proved to me that as long as you have the will and ability to keep putting one foot in front of the other, you would eventually make it from point A to point B, even if point B wasn't exactly what you planned on. The adventure of the unknown, the presence of beauty, encountering nature, and even the joy found in suffering for a satisfying outcome - these are the things draw me to the outdoors. Getting in shape is a nice byproduct, but certainly not the goal.

Though in this instance, I did expect getting in shape was going to make it easier. Having never been in excellent shape, I was only guessing of course. The thru hikers certainly made it seem so. My hiker legs were supposed to change things.

So being almost four weeks in and still experiencing every day as a battle felt disheartening, to say the least. Discouragement makes you lose perspective. Your mind turns all negative and you lose sight of what's good. Growth and progress are no longer in the scales of your judgment, so the gavel comes down with the proclamation of "loser." The truth was it was getting easier because I was doing more miles. It was the extra miles that gave each day its feel of equal suffering.

I think life is often like that.

For each of the 50 days of this hike, I had the idea to reflect on each year of my life. This trip was about celebrating turning 50, so what better way to honor being on the planet 50 years than to recognize each year? It turned out to be way more difficult than I expected. On day 13 I would remind myself to contemplate being a 13 year old, only to balk at remembering such a ghastly age.

But thinking about my 20's actually helped me, even though that decade was exhausting. Giving birth three times before it was even half over, the entirety of the '90s was mostly a fog. I never felt like I was doing a good job. Though because my job kept getting harder, it only felt like I wasn't improving. I kept growing stronger, even if I couldn't see it. Hopefully, I was a better mother than I give myself credit for; and even if I was a bit of a mess, they were good, beautiful years. And hard...very hard.

So for the following days, I decided to "embrace the suck" as they say; and even more importantly, stop berating myself. My attitude improved. Instead of obsessing about the end goal, I focused on day 33 - "Inn Day." Remember the year the kids all went to school? That's what I imagined day 33 would be like. Put your head down, do what you need to do, and know that relief is coming.

My stay at the "Inn at Long Trail" was pre-planned, though I did not send supplies, nor did I have a reservation. When I had called before leaving Washington to ask them questions, the receptionist assured me I was okay being a walk-in and explained that most hikers didn't send supplies, but instead went into town to get what they needed. A two dollar bus that stopped right in front of the inn made it easy. The more I thought about inn day, which I did a lot, the more I hated the idea of spending my precious resting hours at Walmart. My husband would just have to send a box. I didn't care if it was full of Top Ramen and Skittles and cost $40 to ship, it would be worth it to be able to do nothing for the better part of that day. I reworked my plan for the umpteenth time so that I only had to do five miles before getting to the inn. This screwed up my grand ambitions to be caught up on that day, but I believed it was going to be worth it.

Then I realized I was almost out of white gas again. Grrr-rr...that is something that cannot be shipped. Being aware now that if my book relayed that gas was sold somewhere, it did not mean they sold what I needed, I scanned each and every note and finally found a small store not too far off-trail that sold "gas by the ounce." Saved from the horrors of Walmart, I gave the go-ahead for Ken to pack a box full of whatever he felt would be good trail food, and to throw in a new pair of Superfeet for good measure.

I camped practically on the trail that night. With no signs to make me feel guilty, it felt worth the risk to pass the turnoff to the shelter and go an extra half mile. It may seem ridiculous, but with the shelter being almost a half mile off trail, shooting for the upcoming stream and hoping for a flat spot to save myself a wasted mile and get me a little jump on the next day was what I considered a deserving chance to take. The worst case would be having to go back to the shelter. Reaching the stream when the light was fading and finding absolutely nothing, I knew the solution of backtracking was not happening. There would have to be a bear holding an "I'm going to eat you" sign for me to even consider taking another step. The spot on the trail that was slightly wide enough for me to put up my tent and still allow others to pass by was going to be good enough.

As I was barely waking up in the morning, I heard footsteps. Even though I was embarrassed to be practically blocking their way, I called out a question, "Do you know what the forecast is today?"

The response was curt and condescending as if I was an idiot for not already knowing. Even though I couldn't see them, there was no question in my mind it was the European Snobs. I gloried in the fact that I somehow got ahead of them, gram heavy boots and all. Finding out I didn't have to worry about rain was just a bonus.

There's a good chance it rained anyway, I don't remember, but it seemed to rain just about every other day. Except these deluges were becoming shorter and shorter. I started to almost look forward to them; like a midday rinse off. Anything for some relief from the hot, humid air - which for this day was over 100 with the heat index. The reason I know this is because Walter Cummings noted it in his blog from August 29th, which I just finally looked up.

Hiking Lingo Term #11 Trail Magic: Any random act of kindness that is offered or provided to thru-hikers.

Before explaining Walter, I first want to explain more about trail magic. Who can say for certain when the term was coined, though it is generally accepted that it began on the AT. Reading about it in my early researching frenzy, I dared to hope I might experience it once or twice. It was a wonderful surprise to come across some magic on almost a weekly basis.

But unfortunately, humans like to overdo a good thing. This well intentioned benevolence is starting to become a burden for those who maintain the trails, or so I've read. When garbage is left for other people to clean up, or when a large hiker feed causes too many people to hang around in mass, it can become a problem. Hopefully, folks will reign it in - it would be a shame for trail magic to lose its spell.

As usual, I was tempting fate with my low water supply when I saw a cooler marked as trail magic in the parking lot before my final push for the day up Bromley Mountain. Inside was Gatorade or beer. For my extremely parched self on this sweltering day, this magic felt more like a miracle. I'll confess...I nearly went for the ice cold beer. It seems contrary to logic that alcohol would be dehydrating, doesn't it? But facts are facts; one of them being despite how tempting the beer looked, I'd be an idiot to pass on the Gatorade. Just as I was cracking it open, Walter approached me.

Because the sign on the cooler said, “For thru-hikers, not bears,” I immediately felt guilty when Walter explained the drinks were on him, and had to confess I wasn’t a thru-hiker.

“Oh no, don’t worry, I didn’t mean section hikers weren’t welcome. It’s just I am luring the thru-hikers, because of my blog. I drive down to Georgia to meet some of them when they are starting, then I try to find them again as they are getting close to the end. I’m an artist, you see. I draw their portraits and tell their stories. I’m not having much luck this year though. I haven’t come across anyone I met in Georgia yet.”

Wouldn’t you know at that exact moment a thru-hiker named Noodle who Walter recognized appeared out of nowhere. It was sweet to witness their reunion, except for all my outsider insecurities wanting to plague me again.

“Do you seriously think they should care about your piddly 500 miles? Are you sad nobody’s going to draw your picture? Boohoo, how pathetic. You’re lucky to even be enjoying one of their refreshments.”

Nobody said it was easy...especially getting out of your head. Sometimes you lose a battle here and there, and a stupid discouraging thought slips in. But the key can be as simple as seeing that negative voice as an annoying little fly you can shoo away. As long as you don’t get stuck on the thought, it’s over, and you move on. Which I did, right after assuring myself I wasn't pathetic, and then giving a sincere "thank you" to Walter for his miraculous magic.

Only two miles to the top of this snowless ski resort and I would be done. Another day closer to inn day. My book noted a “ski warming lodge” that supposedly was open to hikers, but

I was nervous. What if it was locked? Maybe I should play it safe and stop at the shelter that was a mile before the top. As I weighed my options, I was relieved to see a south bounder coming my way. Unlike the North-going Zax, I was always glad to see my counterpart coming toward me (maybe too obscure of a Dr. Seuss reference, but somebody will appreciate it) because these meetings could bring a wealth of information. In exchange for my letting him know he'd better hurry if he wanted a cold beer, he let me know the ski hut was indeed open and looked like a great place to stay. No water though, he warned, then added there was a small stream less than a half mile from the top. No need to haul all that weight from the only noted water source at the shelter. Thank God, because Guthook's already warned me how steep that last mile was going to be.

There is steep, and then there is ski run steep. Getting up that last half mile felt nearly impossible, even without the extra pounds of water. That's right, I never found the secret stream. I should have known when a thru-hiker tells you there is an un-noted source of water, it means you need a degree in water divining. Reminding myself that "Naked and Afraid" survivalists go a couple of days without water sometimes, I told myself it would be okay. No good meal, possible cramping, and dry mouth...but hey, nobody said it was easy.

LITTLE WATER AND LITTLE FOOD EQUALS A LITTLE NUTS

You would think dehydration would at least yield the benefit of not having to get up and pee in the middle of the night. It may be the thing I hate most about backpacking. Waking up this night was a little different because I wasn't in a tent. The ski warming hut was nicer than expected, but then again, my expectations were not much higher than "I hope there aren't any rats." It was similar in looks to a fire lookout, with lots of windows and a couple of tables. The sink gave me a flicker of hope my water problems were solved, though of course, it was nonoperational, along with the outlets that taunted me with their lack of charging power. A bathroom was nowhere in my realm of expectation, but realizing that I needed to go open the door and squat outside the building felt very odd. The witching hour was ominously dark and rainy and made me hate the idea of getting up to pee even more than usual.

It also felt strange waking and remembering I had company. A south bounder named Spicy had joined me about an hour after I arrived. Another kid avoiding getting a job after college; it was a common theme. I swear it was the answer I got every time I asked anyone who was under 30 why they decided to do this trail. One might judge them for avoiding responsibility, but I was impressed with their honesty and humor. Us old farts can easily fall into "everything is going to hell" when it comes to the younger generation - hasn't it been that way since the dawn of time? But despite all the jokes about the self-entitled millennials, I still have faith in them. I think they are a tougher bunch than we, or they, realize.

Not wanting to wake Spicy, I tried to find my headlamp without making too large a racket, with little success. Then suddenly a light was shining around the room - my half asleep brain could not make sense of it. Was my headlamp on my head and somehow just came on?

Nope, it wasn't my headlamp. It was coming from outside. We had another visitor. I watched as the headlamp came up to the door and the intruder clamored to get inside. Making a racket was obviously of no concern, but who could blame him? This was one hell of a night to be hiking; getting out of the weather must have been a huge relief.

"Hi there!" I greeted cheerfully. Nobody gets that kind of reception if I've just woken up (ask my kids) so the dehydration must have made me delirious. "Wow, I'm glad I wasn't outside peeing when you got here. You would have scared the bejesus out of me!"

Who talks about urinating to a complete stranger who barges in during the middle of the night? I'll blame the delirium. Continuing to ramble on as if this guest had come for dinner, I pointed to a sleeping area Spicy and I had left vacant for just this occasion...except this individual only stood there dripping and didn't seem to be listening to a word I was saying.

"Where's the trail?" he abruptly asked. "For a southbounder, I mean. It's so dark and stormy out, I couldn't find it."

In my mentally imbalanced state, I tried my best to explain, without questioning why in the world he needed to know this minute. It didn't occur to me that he intended to continue hiking, which is exactly what he did. Who does that?

People attempting to break records, that's who. Not until I met a Long Trail hiker (I'll tell you about "Polar Bear" in the next chapter) did I understand why this incomer blasted in and then suddenly out again like a maniac.

At 273 miles in length, the Long Trail spans the length of Vermont and shares 100 miles with the AT - the section I was on during this encounter. Like every trail, it entices those who want to make a name for themselves into seeing if they can do it faster than anyone else. Polar Bear knew what was going on in the Long Trail's news, and when I related this story to her, she was sure this surprise visitor must have been the current contender going for the record. The astoundingly fast four days, 12 hours, and 46 minutes (set in 2009) still stands; so sadly, our fleeting guest that evening was unable to make a name for himself. Maybe next year...when he doesn't have a crazy, dehydrated old lady giving him directions back to the trail.

Spicy offered me some of his water before I left in the morning - another reason not to lose hope in his generation. Despite the evening's downpour, the bowl, and pot I had put out to collect rain produced barely a few ounces. My maps showed three miles before reaching the next water source, so I was incredibly thankful for his kindness.

Having not come upon a single hiker all morning, I was surprised to see someone ambling towards me once I finally stopped to take a break at the long-awaited stream. Even more surprisingly, this guy looked familiar. Skinnier, and sporting a new haircut, but I still recognized good old Pack Rat.

"Hey, you're going the wrong way!" I teased, even though it was true. Obviously, he must know he was headed south, or at least I assumed so. This is when Pack Rat explained his fall. Landing his knee cap straight on a rock, he was lucky to not have broken it; but still, he was mostly incapacitated. Faithfully determined to try to finish, he was staying at the nearby Green Mountain House and slackpacking - though he admitted with the pain he was having, he doubted he'd be able to continue.

> *Hiking Lingo Term #12 Slackpack: Thru-hiking without your backpack while someone transports it to your end destination for the day, or keeps it at the hostel or home where the hiker is staying while being transported to and from the trail each day.*

I had read about slackpacking...it sounded a lot like cheating. Even so, I knew the majority of thru-hikers do it at some point, and in this area, in particular, it was the norm. It's gotten so popular that it's become quite the local industry, and many hostels will compete for business by giving free rides to and from the trail. Going either north or south doesn't really matter in these cases - it depends mostly on what is easiest for the shuttle drivers.

Pack Rat's exuberance over the fabulousness of the boarding house he was staying at made me pretty jealous. It all sounded so very tempting; except how could I justify such blatant chicanery when I was only doing 500 miles? No, as much as I wanted to ask him the number to this magical place, I felt I needed to finish this with my pack on. It would take me another 12 days to give in to the sacrilege of slackpacking.

I wished Pack Rat good luck as he limped away, and believed the worst of my day was behind me. The miles ahead didn't look too bad, plus I had enough water this time to get me by. The upcoming Baker's Peak appeared to be barely a bump by Guthook's standards - I'm sure that's why it felt so hard. Expectations for something easy always ramp up any suffering.

Looking up Baker's Peak now, the description I find is for a "fun rock scramble to great views." Funny, I'm sure anybody watching me scrambling would never use the word "fun" to express what they were witnessing. Cursing the trail and everyone involved in creating it, I couldn't believe I was yet again being forced to rock climb so I could see the same damn rolling hills.

"This view is BULLSHIT," I screamed into the valley below. These outbursts always shocked me. Up until the explosion, I think I'm fully in control. Angry, yes. Annoyed, yes. But crazy? Just a few days earlier I had dumped out the entirety of my toiletry bag all over the trail in a complete fit. That tantrum had hit without warning. I was seemingly normal, sitting down to eat a beef jerky stick. Pulling, pulling, pulling with my teeth. This specific brand was so hard to open - sealed so tight that the more I tried, the harder it cinched down. No problem, I'll just use my fingernail clippers. When I couldn't find them, suddenly I was going entirely ape shit...even going so far as to kick my pack several times. After it was over and I was calmly eating my beef jerky, I thought to myself, "I should probably be eating more snacks."

So here I was, roaring out into the wilderness once again. I reminded myself it was time to sit down and eat some nuts or something. Getting my phone out to give myself a little Snapchat reprieve, I opened one from a dear friend who had made a several minutes long motivational speech for me.

She meant well. She wanted to encourage me - give some helpful advice. Something about if I keep smiling, even if I didn't feel like it, I'll feel more positive. I'm sure it's true. In another time and place, it may have been very beneficial. At that moment...not so much. It's difficult to embrace any advice given by someone who you don't feel can fully understand what you are going through. Sort of like when my male doctor grabbed my face in an effort to aid me during my labor with the helpful instructions to "stop screaming." He's lucky to be alive.

I resisted the urge to throw my phone off the cliff, finished my nuts, and kept on keeping on. Just a few more miles to Big Branch Shelter, and I'd be on track for the inn on day 33. I may have even cracked a smile thinking about it.

OUTSIDER VERSUS INSIDER

If there was ever a night I felt like an obvious outsider, this was it.

When I arrived at Big Branch, I set my tent up in a very small flat spot right next to the shelter, because I could. Counting my blessings for having the whole place to myself, I spread out my cooking gear inside the shelter and enjoyed the view of the river while I dined on another meal of Top Ramen with nasty homemade dehydrated chicken.

My guide book noted this to be a very popular spot, so I wasn't surprised when a small group of hikers showed up. Explaining they were with a hiking group from Williams College, I understood more would be coming soon. I looked at my spot just feet away and felt like I was encroaching on their party, but they assured me I was fine. With a little more small talk, I collected my stuff and scurried inside my tent to hide.

Then the "more" came trickling in...and trickling...and trickling. There had to be 20 or more students; everyone knowing each other, laughing together, working in unison for this grand backpacking experience. And then there was me...right smack in the middle like a giant pimple you try to pretend isn't there, but can't exactly ignore.

Even with all my feelings of awkward discomfort, I'll admit I did hope for a handout. They weren't kidding around with their camp food. With a group that large where everyone can carry something, why not splurge? Instead of little dried bits of chewy weirdness, they had fresh chicken and vegetables they were grilling on their stoves. It smelled amazing. When the smores came out, it was all I could do to not start whimpering.

Of course, I could have gone out there and asked for some - I know they would have gladly shared. Maybe it could have even been a really cool experience, I'll never know. The guilt I felt about the fact I didn't really want to talk or get to know them, but only wanted a gram cracker filled with warm goodness, kept me firmly planted in my sleeping bag. I yearned to be that person who is at ease getting to know everyone and chatting away with funny stories...I wished to be Lightning Rod at that moment, I really did. But I was also okay with accepting I wasn't. I knew trying to prove I wasn't selfish by interacting so I could feel good about eating their food was only going to be painful for everyone.

Thinking about it now, I wished I would have been totally honest, poked my head out of the tent and announced, "I'm too tired and frankly insecure to try and socialize, but would really love to mooch a smore anyway. If someone could just bring it to me, that would be amazing." Wouldn't that have been refreshing? Complete transparency is something I can do on paper, but rarely in real life. I could probably finish the rest of this chapter analyzing why that might be, but that kind of shadow work is perhaps best done in private.

I may have missed out on the delicious food that night, but I got the best breakfast of the trip that morning. No, not from the hiking club; you know I high tailed it out of there as fast as I could. Chris the trail angel was parked at the first road I came to, with hash and eggs cooking on his griddle, along with an entire fold up table loaded with free treats to take with you.

Chris spends a couple weeks out of his summer camping in this spot so that he can feed the hikers. Nobody could complain that this magic was out of control and bad for the environment, with garbage sacks responsibly awaiting any trash and a truck available to haul it all away. He had everything set up so organized and neat, complete with a sign as you approached so you knew what you were coming into:

"Are you hungry? Keep moving stinky freeloaders! Trail Magic Ahead!!!"

I had to laugh when I saw it. The last three words were all decorated with polka dots; like something you'd see for an eight year old's lemonade stand. Having snarky humor juxtaposed with childlike embellishments gave me insight into this benefactor's personality; and sure enough, he was exactly what I imagined. Funny and sweet, with a guileless kind of enthusiasm to be serving others, Chris made the best kind of angel. He inspired me to try and do this in my home state for the PCT hikers. Hopefully, I can live up to his wings.

This day was chock-full of day hikers, and I could see why. A relatively easy grade to the top of the aptly named White Rocks Mountain brought you to a wonderland. Over who knows how many years, people have taken the bountiful white rocks found there and created the most magical city of cairn art I have ever seen.

> *Hiking Lingo Term #13 Cairn: A pile of rocks used to indicate a route. A cairn can be either large and elaborate, or as simple as a small pile of rocks. To be effective, it has to noticeable and obviously man-made.*

Go onto any hiking forum and you will find all kinds of debates about cairns. Even though these piles of rocks have been created since prehistoric times as memorials and landmarks, many naturalists have an issue with them, especially when they are used only artistically. I've read some of the debates about how they alter nature, and nobody could argue the fact that of course the White Rocks Mountain has been altered greatly by the huge imaginative display of rocks piled on it. I say it's been altered for the better. Bring on the cairns! I think they are beautiful, but as trail markers, they can seriously be essential to survival. More about that later.

Some environmentalists may applaud, but I am embarrassed to say that I accidentally knocked down some of this art that day. Trying to stealthily squeeze past a large group of kids listening to their instructor giving a speech (possibly about the evils of piling up rocks just for the heck of it, who knows?) I, of course, made a scene when my pack caught an edge and down came a whole heap. Oops. Let's just say I didn't stay to apologize.

I met Polar Bear as soon as I was safely away from staring eyes and sitting down to eat my lunch...or maybe it's better to say she met me. Polar Bear met everybody. That's who she is, a meet and greeter. In the few hours I spent with her over the course of the next day, she seemed to know almost everybody - and she had only been on the trail a week! How is that possible?

We spoke briefly but warmly, and then she continued on her way while I finished my lunch. Near the end of the day, I found a bandana on the ground I believed to be hers and seeing that she wasn't too far ahead, I rushed ahead to catch her. She had several bandanas tied to her pack, so when she told me this one I had so gallantly rescued for her did not belong to her, I was pretty surprised. After an awkward few seconds standing there at the road while we were waiting for a chance to cross, she made a confession.

"Before you came up behind me, I was seriously thinking about sticking my thumb out and calling this thing quits," she told me, "but you sort of startled me out of it. Like you were a sign to help me continue."

"Well, I'm glad," I answered with a grin, "even though I really didn't do anything."

This was the first time I hiked with anyone for any distance at all. We walked and talked until the hill got too steep, then she wanted to take a break. We were both headed to the same shelter, so I told her I'd see her there.

Terrified she was going to catch up and pass me, I kicked it into major high gear. It was the silliest thing. I knew she'd only just started the Long Trail, was not in great shape, and was obviously struggling to even keep going...so the thought of still getting passed and having to watch her fly up the hill ahead of me, like I did every other hiker, was too much to bear.

"If she passes me, I'm the one who is going to be hitchhiking out of here first thing tomorrow," I grumbled to myself while huffing up that mountain as fast as I could. It was as if my pride had its clutches around my neck, threatening to choke me out.

Pride is a complicated concept, and therefore a word that brings up conflicting emotions and ideas. Being taught to never be prideful makes you wonder how you can ever feel good about goals, achievements, or self-discovery. Obviously, I'm not speaking of the kind of pride that adds value to the human experience. The pride that NEEDS to be better than others in order to have its own value is the kind that is a killer. It HAS to win because it fears losing, fears judgment, fears vulnerability. It will hide the truth to uphold an image that others will see as more worthy, even though it's a lie. It won't even ask for a smore because appearances are more important...more important than even warm gooey chocolate.

Though pride did get me up that hill in a hurry; I have to give it that.

Polar Bear arrived long after me, which of course made my pride exceeding happy. She hobbled over to the shelter where I was cooking my dinner and blurted out how she had already stopped to eat earlier because she needed a long rest before finishing that ghastly last half mile. My pride winced. So that was the reason she didn't pass me? But here's the thing - that ugly pride couldn't keep its grasp on me in the presence of Polar Bear's light. Her unpretentious, bubbly, open and loving demeanor melted me. I even felt safe enough to confess how much

I needed to beat her, and we laughed.

As we were comparing our pictures of the beautiful art stacks that we both agreed now only looked like a bunch of rocks on our phone screens, "Mazlo" showed up. He fit right in...or maybe it was Polar Bear's spell that made it so. We told stories. Out came the blueberry beer someone had given her that day, and she shared it with us. (Of course, complete strangers would give her a big fancy bottle of ale. Why wouldn't they?) We toasted to our separate and yet common adventure.

If there was ever a night I felt I obviously belonged, this was it.

PHILOSOPHY AND DELI MEATS

Hiker Lingo Term #14 Hiker Family or "Tramily": A group of hikers that stick together and become very close as a result of their shared experiences along the trail.

I had a hiker family for all of about six hours. It was surprising and marvelous to even get a small taste of an experience I had completely ruled out as impossible for a speed impaired non-thru-hiker like myself. Surely Maslow, as the only thru-hiker between us, slowed his pace so we could walk and talk together; though he was the one doing most of the talking, so it worked out for everybody.

At one point he was describing his strategy for tired legs which he called the penguin walk. Yep, it was exactly as it sounds, and for the life of me I couldn't figure out how it could possibly help with anything. By the look Polar Bear gave me as he was demonstrating it, she couldn't either.

Somehow we went from penguin walking to talking philosophy. Maslow had explained the night before about getting his trail name from "Maslow's hierarchy of needs" - a psychological theory I had never heard of before, thus he was now describing it in more detail. In short, your basic needs for food, water, and shelter need to be met before you can pursue the higher goals of love and belonging. This seemed a bit of a "no shit Sherlock" theory, but Polar Bear was taking some issue it. Unfortunately, I can't recall the specifics of their argument - I was far too busy concentrating on keeping up with them. But I do remember it was good natured and fun to listen to. In the end, I landed mostly on Polar Bear's side.

We used to sing a song in church, "Seek ye first the kingdom of God, and it's righteousness, and all these things will be added unto you, hallelu, hallelujah." Love and belonging first, and then things will fall into place. Counterintuitive to the survival brain for sure, as most of Jesus' teachings are. Confusion over the "kingdom of God" aside, (and the fear of not making it in) I see the truth in it. By the way Polar Bear was getting by, it did seem to be working well for her.

Hearing about her trail name was far less confusing, and much more humorous. It was easy to imagine the scene as she described herself jibbering away to the group of hikers she came upon after reaching camp on her 2nd or 3rd day.

"I was just so nervous I kept talking; telling them all about my experience thus far. I had tried to hang my bear bag the first night and did a horrible job. I couldn't get it down. So I was going on and on about how I had to climb the tree to get my bag down."

This is where she started laughing just thinking about the memory and had to pause before continuing, "I kept saying, 'I was like a polar bear going up that tree, you should have seen me, climbing like a polar bear,' and then it occurred to me that polar bears aren't doing a lot of tree climbing." We all laughed as she finished, "I felt so stupid, but luckily the guys thought I was funny, and then one announced in his thick Ukrainian accent, 'You will be Polar Bear'."

Now that's a trail name tale that is hard to come by. Beats the Apple story by a mile.

Before we knew it, we were at the road crossing where Loretta's was only a half mile away. This is the store I had read sold white gas, but because they also sold sandwiches, our little family migrated together for this last little bit together. Maslow was obsessed with sandwiches and talked about them with more and more fervor the closer we got.

The Yellow Deli was brought up, a place that supposedly had the best sandwiches ever, and he went into great detail as to why. The Yellow Deli is where both he and Polar Bear were headed after we finished lunch at Loretta's. According to Maslow, you can never get enough good sandwiches. The Yellow Deli is a fascinating deviation from your average cafe. Not just a place to eat, but a commune run by the Twelve Tribes, it is a staple with the thru-hikers as a cheap hostel. When I read about it in my guidebook, I considered staying there, but ultimately chickened out. It sounded weird. After talking to Maslow and Polar Bear, I realized my instincts were correct. But hey, if you are into good sandwiches, you don't care if it is run by a cult.

Walking and talking along VT-103, Polar Bear was busy updating her social media. By the time we reached Loretta's, she had a ride to Yellow Deli all lined up. Get this - a couple (that she JUST MET on the trail the day before) saw her post on Instagram as they were driving a little further down the same highway. They made a u-ie and lickety-split appeared at Loretta's ready to drive Polar Bear wherever she needed to be. Love and belonging baby...that is where it is at.

Maslow and I also benefited from Polar Bear's charm. Lucky enough to be within her circle of enchantment, we both got a lift as well. First I got dropped off back at the trail, then they would head to Yellow Deli to resist indoctrination, while simultaneously enjoying the finest of deli meats.

Loretta's did not sell white gas, by the way. Antifreeze...that supposedly is just as good. All the hikers use it, they told me. That night I had to eat another God-forsaken meal of protein bars because I couldn't get my stove to work. Protein bars suck, in case you didn't know, and the more you eat the worse they get.

The AT Guide notes for the following day spoke of a chair-lift that took you to a restaurant. Killington Peak is a ski resort during the winter but caters to bikers during the summer. Many ski resorts are operational for both seasons due to mountain bikers, which in turn yields benefits for the hiking community as well. I was super excited for the restaurant of course, until reading further and discovering it was a very steep half mile off-trail to the lift, and then I would have to hand over a twenty for it to take me to the restaurant. I had ruled it out, but now that I didn't have a working stove, I had to reconsider. Getting something in my belly besides protein bars had become a priority even above being cheap and lazy.

Finding out the restaurant was actually at the chair lift was a huge relief to my tightwad mentality, and the amazing food there was a literal lifesaver. Okay, not literally. Using that word when you don't actually mean it has become a pet peeve of mine. Death was not inevitable had I not gotten a delicious hot hoagie (I suppose Maslow had inspired my order) especially considering another good meal was just around the corner...in a figurative and not literal way. Day 33 would be here, come morning light, and along with it my heavily anticipated stay at the Inn at Long Trail.

This is why I wasn't too concerned about my stove, though knowing I'd have to head to Walmart, after all, to get actual white gas was a huge disappointment. Oh well, at least I could buy myself another cheap bottle of wine. Sitting in a bathtub for hours and drinking the whole thing sounded like a perfect plan.

As I was lost in bubble bath daydreams and nearing my last shelter stay before blessed inn day, I ran into a hiker who had become somewhat of a legend for the 2018 AT season. I wished that I had wanted to meet him, but I had actually been warned to be somewhat on guard. "Tighty Whitie Guy" had been accused of making women hikers feel uncomfortable, and not just because he insisted on wearing only his briefs. Nothing overt or harassing, I was told, but he was odd enough to make a person suspicious.

"Hey, Tighty Whitie Guy!" was my way of being indiscrete. I don't know what's wrong with me, I think I was just nervous. At least he gave a little laugh, then was quick to correct me about his real trail name, which I don't recall because Tighty Whitie Guy was so much better. He explained that he just wants to be comfortable and feels best in his underwear. He seemed genuine about not meaning to offend. Still, I was thankful he said he was going on to Killington instead of the shelter I was headed to.

Considering my impatience and readiness to be done with this day, reaching the shelter was far less excruciating than usual. Never underestimate the power of a good sandwich.

Waking up on day 33 was like another Christmas morning. Just five and a half miles, then I could open my presents. Looking at Guthook's, I could see that once I got to Hwy 4, I could simply turn right and road walk a mile, bypassing the three AT miles that went up and around to the backside of the inn. Time to cash in my last cheater mile chips! Not even a hesitation.

The road walk made me think of my little lost hiker family. Christmas would be so much more joyous with them around. Polar Bear had mentioned she was hoping to stay at the Inn at Long Trail, so I was crossing my fingers I'd see her there. I had a feeling I'd be buying her a beer before the day was over.

GOING UNDER DOESN'T MEAN STAYING UNDER

Sitting in the lobby of the Long Trail Inn and opening the box of supplies Ken had sent did not generate the yuletide spirit I had envisioned. Sure, I was pleased as punch to be there, and I knew the new Superfeet insoles were going to be a game changer. But not having anyone to laugh with over the two pounds of candy Ken considered good trail food, or to kiss for the small bottle of Fireball, brought with it a loneliness that was hard to endure.

On top of this were thoughts of my youngest daughter, who would be turning 18 in about 14 hours. This didn't help with my feelings of sadness at all. What kind of mother abandons her kid on such a momentous birthday? Trying to distract myself from the guilt and heartache, I went to ask again how the bus schedule worked.

Every other hour the bus came in the direction I was headed, so it wasn't long before I was on my way to Rutland. Bus drivers aren't often looked upon with much respect; they are part of the millions of workers who fulfill positions we take for granted on a daily basis. Observing him as he did his job, he made me realize how marvelous it is when you take pride in your employment, regardless if it is honored by society or not. He treated me as his guest for those 20 minutes, with welcome and care. As he picked up his regulars, they were all greeted like friends. These were folks you knew didn't have the easiest row to hoe in life, and you could see how much being treated with respect and dignity meant, even if only for a short ride. Pride is beautiful when it flows out from yourself and into everyone around you.

I made it back to the inn even before my room was ready, with gas and wine and several subway sandwiches in hand. (Still under some weird mind control by Maslow, apparently. He should start his own cult.) In the time I had yet to wait for my bath fantasies to come true, I kept myself occupied in a corner of the parking lot making sure my stove only needed it's proper gas to be operational. After an hour, I had to accept this was not the case. My stove was shot. Bath nirvana would need to stay on hold until I figured out where the bus would need to take me next.

Normally I would be extremely upset about wasting this time and having to fork out $70 for a new stove, though somehow this day had miraculously wrapped its arms around me in a spirit of gratitude. From the friendly bus drivers, to the shining sun, to the helpful outfitter just down the road, to the opportunity to spend time talking on the phone with my family and especially my daughter - everything felt right with the world. Right up to when I dropped my phone in the bath, that is.

Drinking wine while snapchatting in the tub with my husband turned out to be maybe not the best decision ever. I tried not to freak out, I mean, it did seem to still be working. When it refused to charge, panic was inevitable. To keep myself from spiraling, I made bad choice #2 to head to the bar to drown my sorrows, as if I wasn't already half way under.

Actually, I'm grateful for that portion of the day too. If I would have stayed in my room and sulked, I may not have connected with Polar Bear again. We bellied up together, and I bought her that foreseen beer. Lightning Rod even made an appearance - it was practically a hiker reunion. I'm afraid by the time I was buying everyone an extra round, I was completely under. But thanks to the extra alcohol pushing me into the obnoxious zone, my loud complaints about my soggy Samsung were heard by the nearby table of Long Trail hikers, who told me they had some extra rice they would gladly give me to help dry it out.

I'm going to add another confession here, just incase anyone goes to watch my Youtube videos and sees the one where I discribe how I never saw LR again that night. The truth is, I have no recollection of seeing him. But apparently he was there, and I introduced him to Polar Bear and everything. I know this now because Polar Bear and I kept in touch, and she even stayed with me for a couple days while she was on a cross country road trip. It was then that she filled me in on parts of this night that had been lost to me. So when I say I went under, I mean way under.

But regardless of my inebriated state, by the end of the night, my phone was resting in a bag of that generously donated rice, and it actually worked to dry out my phone. By day 34 all was well with the world once again...except with a raging headache.

Before leaving in the morning, I paid that bag of rice forward to the illustrious hiker box, along with my own donation.

Hiker Lingo Term #15 Hiker box: A box kept at hiker locations wherein hikers can leave their unwanted items and pick up other hikers' unwanted items.

This is where I left my 1.5 pounds of candy, amidst the many assorted bottles of sunscreen and shrimp flavored Top Ramen. I discarded several items in these boxes along the way, including my superfluous wall chargers and a favorite mug. I have hope they all found good homes.

Something else I had to depart with at this time was my beloved Polar Bear. The Long Trail and the Appalachian Trail part ways at this point, and therefore so did we. Of all the hikers I met, she is the only one I know for certain completed her goal. Instagram showed me the rest of her journey; filled, of course, with pictures of the many new friends she made. It was an honor I got to be one of them.

I was all alone again that night. These sharp contrasts between being social and being solitary would mess with my equilibrium. Suddenly I was jumpy again - spooked. When I heard a hiker come in late, it gave me a measure of peace. To see it was Maslow, barely out of his sleeping bag as I was already packed up and leaving in the morning, gave me regret for not having a chance to chat. But like I said, my pack was on, and once that happens, visiting hours are over. The young ones like Maslow could afford to be late sleepers, unlike me with my 50 year old legs. If Pack Rat was right, I still had another week before my legs would be fully upgraded. With 160 miles still ahead of me, I needed all the help I could get.

I did get a chance to visit a little with Maslow a couple of days later. He appeared as I was eating lunch by a stream, so while he got himself some water, we had a few minutes to talk.

The mystery of how I could possibly be ahead of him was solved when he explained how his late starts were now a daily routine. It was obvious how difficult it became to keep the resolve and drive up the closer to Katahdin the thru-hikers got. How could it not? To keep pushing day after day for a full half year (the average time it takes to complete the AT) takes a kind of willpower few can generate. The latest statistics state only 20% are successful, so I can only have faith Maslow made it; which I fully do.

When describing to him my dilemma of where to camp that night, he was kind enough to direct my attention to a feature on Guthook's that I had ignored. This was the "info" section, where hikers basically chatted about anything they thought others might find helpful. When I first met Little Debbie and Gaucho, they asked how I had faired with a heavily flooded crossing that everyone was "talking" about on Gut-hook's. As luck would have it, I avoided doing the several mile alternative road detour that was advised because I didn't know any better. Somehow I managed to get across - probably because the water receded just enough to be able to scramble over the large branches that had collected in that spot. The girls were very unhappy to hear that they had done all those road miles for nothing ("the worst part of the day," they said) and I decided being blissfully ignorant was in my best interest.

Though this info section had much more to offer, like actual phone numbers of folks in town who were willing to put you up. Maslow suggested a church he had heard was open to hikers, so I thanked him and quickly added the contact in my phone. He talked a little more about deli meats, I'm not even joking, then away he went - sadly, never to be seen again. Happy trails and sandwiches to him.

Just the other day I read an article about this sharing aspect of Guthook's, and how it was recently used to keep everyone abreast of the location of an erratic and aggressive hiker who was amongst the 2019 hiker crowd. Everyone knew he was mentally imbalanced and a danger; but sadly, it didn't help. Eventually, he stabbed a fellow hiker to death and left another critically wounded. It makes me wonder...would I have preferred being naive about the presence of this mad man had I been hiking this year? Maybe it seems foolish, but I almost think I would want my "blissfully ignorant" strategy in this case. Averting the terror of constantly thinking about where he might be outweighs being savvy, in my mind anyway.

All that heavy pondering aside, I was grateful for the insight on a different option for a place to lay my head that night. I dialed the number almost before Maslow was out of view. The stream I had hoped would provide a flat enough spot for my tent was only a mile outside of Norwich, and when I came to it I saw zilch in the way of anything remotely camp worthy. What a relief that plan B was already arranged. The only reason I had hoped I could stealth camp at the stream was because I didn't want to pay the $150 at what I thought was the only option in the tiny upcoming town. The Norwich Inn would have been a wonderful treat I could not afford, (especially after buying everyone drinks at the inn) but for the small price of a gladly bestowed $20 donation, the St. Barnabas Episcopal Church was an experience I wouldn't have wanted to miss.

AN ASSORTMENT OF DELAYING DISTRACTIONS

I love dramatic tales of fugitives going into a church to claim sanctuary. These stories of asylum sought out by the oppressed have always drawn me. I suppose I had those images in my mind when I pictured the scene of my lone hiker self sleeping by the alter...so theatrical.

St. Barnabus looked the part. A grand old building flaunting large medieval looking doors beneath an impressive steeple; just the kind of place a waif like me should go begging. Though churches and safety have been somewhat of an oxymoron for many; some churches can be downright scary if we are honest. My feelings about the whole thing were definitely mixed. The trepidation kept growing as I awaited the parishioner I spoke with on the phone to arrive and greet me.

Turns out my visions of pew crashing were all wrong. A separate building, complete with a kitchen, classrooms, and bunk beds for weary travelers would be my abode for the night. I guess I wouldn't be curled up under the communion table after all. After the tour of the facilities, I asked the kind couple who had welcomed me how I was to lock the doors. I was answered with a scoffing of, "This is Vermont. We don't do locks."

It's strange how you can go for weeks sleeping in the woods, with nothing but a zipper keeping you from harm's way, to being completely unnerved by the idea of being alone in an unlocked building. Except I knew I wasn't completely alone. The mouse scampering about in the pile of discarded clothes left by past hikers let me know I wasn't the only guest there seeking sanctuary. A proper hiker box for the St. Barnabas wayfarer's suite would be a great addition, just sayin'.

Shockingly, I slept soundly regardless. That's a real benefit of being so physically exhausted; even paranoia can't keep you awake. I chose to take a leisurely morning instead of taking advantage of the time saved from not having to break camp; so after putting a Jackson in the donation box, I decided to go check out the chapel.

The nice man who showed me around the night before had insisted I should take some time to admire the actual sanctuary before I left. He boasted of how it was designed by the famous architect, Hobart Upjohn, in 1917.

Pushing open the unlocked castle-like doors, I felt like an intruder...an imposter even. I had carried a load of contempt for religious institutions for over a decade. Didn't that make me an apostate?

But I sat silently in the pew anyway and considered all the lives of those who had sat there and prayed over the past century. I felt the long history of all of us who search; and yes, I think we've gotten so much wrong. But it's okay. That's what I felt, there in a building that represented so much that I can't stomach anymore. (Though the rainbow flags scattered about did give me a measure of hope.) l have to believe our misunderstandings about God can't keep us from belonging to God, and I know I'm not alone in that understanding. The real sanctuary is found in the depths of our hearts, where we know we are beloved. Sorry, Mr. Upjohn...though your place was a nice place to sit and contemplate these things just the same.

After having such a centering start of the day, I did not expect the reign of confusion that followed. As I hit the road, I noticed my Guthook's maps had run out. Vermont may not need locks, but they could sure use a few more cell towers because service there is terrible. Nothing would download, so my trusty app was once again rendered useless. Being that New Hampshire was less than a mile away, I at least had the hope service would be better once I crossed the Ledyard Free Bridge, and then I could purchase my last set of maps to help steer me through the town. With no obvious trail to follow, street walking was always the most confusing for me.

Once I was in Hanover, not only could I not get my Guthook's to work to help me out, I found myself in a sea of people. Of all days to try and maneuver through a college town, student move-in day has got to be the worst. The small sketches found in my guidebook detailing a few side streets were not enough to prevail against my clouded and confused mind. I needed to find the store where I had sent my last supply package, but I kept getting turned around, as is my nature. Floundering and frustrated, I at last somehow stumbled across it.

Zimmerman's is another outfitter that will hold your shipments at no cost, but you know what they say about getting what you pay for. After shaking all the ants off my disheveled looking box, I at least could relax in seeing it was still intact; and most importantly, my good jacket was now with me. The September weather was changing quickly, so the timing for sending my warm gear ahead was perfect. I had all I needed for my final 12 day push.

My guidebook notes mentioned handouts for hikers at several of the nearby businesses, and even knowing how much I could not afford to waste any more time, I still couldn't resist hunting them down. With the heavy crowds and long lines, focusing so much on free food was a ridiculous endeavor. The slice of pizza I received may have been free, but I paid a high price in time. When I finally made it to the trail leading into the woods at the edge of a ballpark at the far side of town, I knew my cheapskate self had sabotaged any chance for making my goal for the day.

New Hampshire signage was the most explicit yet: "Camping PROHIBITED within 200 feet of this trail" - and yes, prohibited was in caps. Venturing 200 feet into the bush might result in never finding my way back, so I knew sticking with the shelters was going to be pretty important. Too bad it wasn't going to happen; not that day at least.

I called it quits as soon as I found a place where I felt I could be legal without getting lost, even though it was killing me to be stopping early on a day where I had wasted so much time. A mowed path leading toward a house, barely wide enough for my tent, was what I felt might be my only opportunity for a lawful camp spot. It was obviously part of someone's land; a homemade trail they had made with a riding mower. No private property signs though, and because I was quite a distance from the home, I deemed it permissible.

As the last rays of sun were slowly disappearing, I heard something outside my tent. Scratching, sniffing, whining - all the hungry animal noises. It must have been the hard-earned pizza I was, at last, enjoying that had attracted them. I could almost hear their tails wagging. Yep, the farm folk were out taking their dogs for a walk, only to find a squatter blocking their way.

"I hope it's okay I'm here," I whimpered apologetically, then braced myself for harsh words. What a relief when they told me not to worry about it. If I was Lightning Rod they probably would have invited me in for dinner, but I was satisfied just to not be asked to leave.

Looking up what is expected with the "200 feet" rule once I got home, I discovered that using an undesignated spot near the trail, if it is obviously pre-existing, is generally accepted as better than tramping through the forest and causing even more disruption to the environment. All along I felt like this made the most sense, and when I passed one of these obvious areas just two miles from my stupid farmland spot the next morning,

I felt annoyed. Following rules you feel are arbitrary leaves a sour note in your stomach.

Determined to avoid any more emotional conflict over compliance with nonsensical regulations, I pushed hard to make it to the Trapper John Shelter. Quite a few people were on the trail this beautiful weekend day, and as I was passing one of them coming the opposite direction, he stopped me.

"Hey, just a head's up that a mother bear is up there with her cubs. I decided I didn't want to go by her, so I'm going back down to my car. Maybe she'll be gone by the time you get up there, but you might want to head back and avoid her altogether too, just to be on the safe side," he warned.

"Head back where?" I thought. Sure, all these day hikers with cars waiting for them at the trailhead could skedaddle out of there, but I had no clue what I was supposed to do. There was only onward for me, so I just prayed mama bear would be on her way before I reached her, as he suggested she might.

Another couple passed me as they were heading up, and assuming the man had given them the same warning, I jokingly told them to, "scare those bears away for me, will ya?" Not 10 minutes passed before they were headed back toward me in a hurry.

"There is a bear up there! It growled at me! You should not go any further!" she breathlessly admonished as they rushed by. Because of their shock and surprise at seeing a bear, I realized they hadn't already been told about her as I assumed, and must have thought I was only being facetious with my joking. I felt a little guilty for not giving them a proper warning and promptly sat my butt down to ponder what to do.

An elderly woman I had passed earlier caught up to me, but before I could even open my mouth, she let me know she already heard about the bear.

"Are you going to turn around?" I asked her.

"I've completed the AT twice," she announced with pride, "and I've seen plenty of bears. And besides, my husband is waiting in the car on the other side of this mountain to pick me up. I can't go back."

I responded by telling her I couldn't turn around either, but that I thought I would just stay put for a little while. "If I don't hear any screaming, I'll assume you made it past her," I jested as she forged ahead.

It wasn't long before she was back. "Do you have any pots in that backpack of yours?" she asked.

She had a plan that we would go together, I would bang my pots, and that the bear would be scared away. When I asked about the cubs, she pooh-poohed that information as "a bunch of crap. I didn't see any." Her self appointed expertise and assured confidence won me over, so I got out my loudest cooking appliances and marched behind her like a soldier going into battle.

The bear didn't budge. It kept munching away on some berries just 20 feet from the trail like we didn't exist. Keeping our distance, probably 50 feet, we continued with the clamor. Nothing. Either that bear was deaf, or it didn't give two shits about us. I assumed the latter. A bear who is not afraid of humans is a dangerous bear; I thought this is a given.

Although my supposed bear specialist guide did seem somewhat stumped by the bear's indifference, she was not deterred. It's remarkable an old woman, probably 20 years my senior, could make me feel so invincible against a bear attack; but such was the strength of her spirit. We waited, and suddenly the bear bolted up a tree.

"Okay, we can go now," she announced - and away she went as if a traffic light just turned green. I followed like a disciple; squashing any thoughts of doubt popping up in the back of mind that maybe she was just a crazy old lady leading me to my death.

The exhale I eventually gave made me realize I had been holding my breath for quite some time. No bear attack. My hiking guru was legit. With the hiker name of "Mother Nature," who could have doubted?

She told me all about her adventures with her husband, "Father Time," as we hiked together until we reached the turn-off to the next shelter.

"When I do these day hikes, I like to go visit all the shelters. It brings back memories," she explained when she turned to leave. I was sad to see her go, especially since I was still seeing a lot of bear scat on the trail. But my sights were on the next shelter, and I didn't have any time to waste. No more quiet moments in churches, no more waiting in lines for free food, no more quitting early in fear of breaking some ridiculous rule - and God willing, no more waiting around for bears to get out of my way. If I could keep at it, I would be caught up and back on schedule in just two days. I really had a shot at completing my 500 miles if I could just keep my head on straight and follow the plan...for once.

FORCES TO BE RECKONED WITH

"Cried thinking of mom today."

That is it for my notes for day 39. I was a little surprised to find that memory jotted down because I have no recollection of it. It's been almost two decades since she died, so it is not very often that tears come anymore. But obviously, I was feeling extra lonely, and so it's no wonder that thoughts of her would bring the blues.

Actually, it was probably meeting Mother Nature that brought the longing for my own mother. They were similar women - both forces to be reckoned with. (I have a good friend back in Washington who often gets this idiom confused and declares, "I am NOT a force to be reckoned with!" - which always gets her giggles instead of the holy fear she is going for.) Even though my mom never tromped through the woods scaring off bears, she had her ways of being fearless. Humor was always her way of beating down anxiety, and I like to think I learned her lessons well. But as I made camp at the John Trapper Shelter, I did not feel funny, nor brave. Even though I had finally grown used to the many sounds the forest makes, this night I was back to jumping at each nut falling from a tree. Every sound was once again a bear creeping up on me.

I relaxed a little when the sounds became footsteps. The thru-hikers often came in after dark, and it was always a relief to know I wasn't completely alone. "Something else for the bears to eat," I told myself. (There's that humor. If you can laugh, you can calm yourself - it's a very helpful tool.) I didn't let myself wonder if it was Lightning Rod, because I knew I'd be leaving too early to even say hi. And so day 40 started just as lonely as day 39 had ended.

This day brought a serious temperature drop and a new fear. Even with the warmer gear I had just sent myself, I still didn't think I was prepared for truly cold weather. If the rain came while I was up high on the upcoming exposed cliffs, along with the forecasted strong gusts of bone-chilling wind, I was going to be in a world of hurt. My alarm went off even before first light, in hopes I could beat the weather and get to the shelter before it got too bad.

The relief I felt as I approached the large Hexacube Shelter was dampened by more than the rain that had luckily only just started. The wind had been relentlessly assaultive all day, but the air at that shelter was even colder. The hikers already holed up there, huddled in its six corners, gave zero greetings at my arrival. It's not like I was expecting a welcoming committee, I mean I know it had been a crappy day for all; but a hello would have been nice.

I attempted to engage...a little wit, a couple questions...but nothing could penetrate the thick, emanating indifference. I have never come across such a strong wall of apathy; it felt almost hostile. One guy didn't even bother looking up. The whole scene was a display of my worst fears come to life.

After claiming my spot in the deafening silence, I went about making my dinner. Maybe everyone will loosen up a little eventually; maybe the stories and laughter and comradery just needed time? But sadly, the only thing that came that night was the constant sound of rain, and darkness so dense I couldn't see my hand in front of my face. Regardless of having shelter and company, it was the longest, coldest, loneliest night yet. Day

46, with its welcome committee of two people who loved me, could not come soon enough.

Unfortunately, the following day was not looking to be any less of a nightmare. The rain continued, and the sloping granite increased. I was almost to the White Mountains now; as the smooth, slick rocks would attest to. Yet if I could manage to not kill myself by sliding off of one, I believed my luck would soon change. How could the "Hikers Welcome Hostel" not be the happiest place ever? Withstand 15 miles of granite abuse, and then not only would I make my objective and be rewarded with a bed and shower, but I would also make day 41's true goal. That's right - for the first time since my very first night at Wildcat Shelter, I would be somewhere I had originally planned on being ON the day I planned on being there. In other words, I'd be all caught up.

Of course, I was struggling with the "I'm going to jinx it" worry. "Something will go wrong, it always does...you'll never make it...I bet you get lost"...all the thoughts my Eeyore side could muster. If only I could have stayed positive and focused, I probably wouldn't have got lost. Sometimes our thoughts become our own self fulfilled destiny.

Because of all the rocks, there were often cairns used instead of blazes in this area. I managed to make it up and over Mount Cube following them, and thought I had conquered the granite maze. Finally, a sign saying "North," so I turned and followed. Dammit, more rocks and more cairns. I was so focused on getting over the smooth expanses of wet, slick rock without falling on my ass, (which I did several times just the same) it took me far too long to realize I hadn't seen a blaze of any kind in a while.

I quickly looked, and there it was - my Guthook's dot off in neverland. Here we go again; the sick feeling in my stomach, along with all kinds of scenarios of death cycling through my mind. I knew my rational brain had deserted me, and my hysterical brain might not be able to make its way back to the AT, even with Guthook's help. The path I had taken was extremely undefined, so it took every ounce of my resolve to inch my way back, hoping to find where I had made my mistake.

No time to listen to Eeyore anymore. No time to beat myself up for being stupid - or as Stuart Smalley would say, "No more stikin' thinkin'!" This was the time to become my own force to be reckoned with. Don't get me wrong, I was on the very edge of completely losing it. But I didn't. I pulled it together, and for that, I'm proud. Eventually, I made it back to the "North Side" sign - a trail that had nothing to do with the AT. Yes, I had wasted a good hour, but it didn't matter. As long as I didn't hurt myself, I could still make it. I would make it. Please God, I just want to make it.

I must have looked at my phone 10 times when I made my turn on Route 25 towards town. I could hardly believe I had done it. Plus it didn't hurt to be extra, extra sure I was going the right way. Glencliff is not the greatest looking place if I'm honest. As I made my way down the two lane highway, observing each property, I found myself praying, "Please don't be that one."

Knowing nothing about the hostel I was headed to, I was ecstatic when I realized my GPS was leading me to the only place that didn't resemble a crack house. It stands out because of it's new construction, though I quickly realized that was a bit of an illusion. The original homestead that the much prettier addition stems off of is tired and broken down as hell, and of course, that's the only part where the stinky hikers are allowed; but who could expect differently? Not me. I was just happy to be there.

The whole place was buzzing with fellow disheveled, displaced persons. It felt a lot like a summer camp for the homeless. Many of them had their tents set up in the large backyard, but my usually strong cheap ass soul was not robust enough to keep me from splurging on a bed. The host gave me my sheets and said I could pick my own bunk, then pointed me to the other new building - a barn-ish type structure just 40 or so feet away.

"Fill out this form for everything you are purchasing. $30 for the bed, $3 for laundry or shower, and food items are individually priced. You can sign up for slackpacking over on that sheet, which is $15 per person, but at least two people have to sign up for us to do it. As of yet, nobody is on it for tomorrow."

It was all a bit much for my exhausted brain to process. One word quickly implanted though - slackpack. Nothing made me happier than the idea of being free of my backpack for a whole day. Any hoity-toity ideology about it teetering on cheating was long gone. I HAD to find a second person.

With all the other hikers there, you would think this would be easy. It wasn't. Talking folks into things has never been my thing, and it seemed everyone was set on a rest day. I even got scolded for trying to convince "Drop Bear" to come with me. How was I supposed to know he had been unofficially banned from the trail?

When talking to Drop Bear, he did seem slightly off, but I didn't think much of it. A lot of folks are "off" in their own way; maybe even the majority. (Myself included.) Except Drop Bear was not naturally weird like the rest of us. I was later informed he had done some acid (maybe a lot, considering his name) and hence had remained in a state of being a few fries short of a Happy Meal. Nobody knew exactly what to do with him, although everyone was trying to make him stay put until they could reach his family. Being that his home was on a completely different continent, things were complicated; and so Drop Bear had been staying there for almost a week. I was very touched at how everyone was chipping in and helping out to keep him safe - people who barely knew him. On top of all this, someone had to keep informing newbies like me not to entice Drop Bear back into the woods, where everyone was sure he'd never find his way out again.

So after the admonishment to leave Drop Bear be, then seeing the one gal who was considering going with me cross her name off the list, I had to concede that my slackpack dream was dead. Standing there in a state of mourning, staring at my sole name on the hanging sheet of paper, I heard the host come up behind me. "You know you can just pay for two people and go by yourself if you want," she suggested. Slackpack dream alive... cheap ass soul, dead.

BROKE

So, just how much did I end up spending at the Hikers Welcome Hostel, you ask? I left there with less than a twenty to my name. Yes, they would have taken credit, but I figured it was time to get rid of my cash. And let me tell you, with my money monger spirit now crushed, it went fast. My completed form looked something like this:

2 nights w/bed: $60

Shower: $3

Laundry: $3

2 microwave breakfast sandwiches: $5

2 frozen mini pizzas: $10

2 ice cream sandwiches: $5

4 bags of Doritos: $4

5 oz white gas: $3

4 slackpack rides: $60

Total = $153

You're wondering how the slackpack got up to $60, aren't you? I misunderstood that whole part too. I knew I would get a ride to the north end of Moosilauke Mountain, where I would head south the nine miles back to the hostel for my 2nd night's stay. I knew I would need another ride back the following day to the north end, having completed Moosilauke and therefore "skipping ahead" to where I needed to continue with my northern journey. I understood I was paying for two slackpacks, just so I could go at all. What I didn't understand was that the $15 was not for the slackpack experience, but for each ride. Unfortunately, nobody was signed up the following day either, therefore slackpacking turned out to be a far more expensive excursion than I had anticipated.

And worth every penny. My inner Scrooge may have been turning over in her grave, but after facing Moosilauke, I can tell you I would have paid twice that.

It was a much longer ride than I expected. It may have only been a nine mile walk, but to get there by car took over a half hour. The hostel caretaker who was driving me spent most of the time telling me about Drop Bear, and how he was driving him nuts.

"I know he feels bad he can't pay, so he is constantly trying to be helpful, but honest to God he somehow ends up just undoing everything I just did. I don't know what we are going to do; he can't keep staying there. We are not a mental health facility."

After about the 3rd story of various Drop Bear shenanigans, I was glad to see we were finally at the large trailhead parking lot. I was told the north end drop off (instead of pick up at the end of the day) made sense for more than just the convenience of being able to walk back to the hostel at your own pace. Going north to south on this mountain was supposedly far easier.

"It may be easier, but it's not easy. It's steep and slippery. Be sure to watch your step," were my last instructions before he pulled away. A sign I soon came across reiterated the warning:

"This trail is extremely tough. If you lack experience, please use another trail. Take special care at the cascades to avoid tragic results."

As I made my way up the glistening rocks, made eternally wet by the bordering waterfall, all I could feel was complete amazement that anyone would even try coming down them. It was so steep that wooden steps had been bolted in the rock in places (way too far apart in my opinion) and the thought of taking the large steps down the just as slick wood with the weight of my large backpack pulling me forward...well, let's just say I was feeling extremely grateful for the slackpack opportunity. Without it, there is no doubt I would have gone down backward on that part, like a toddler trying to conquer the stairs. Except I'm certain copious swear words and tears would have been included.

I arrived back at the hostel just as the shuttle van was leaving into "town." Even though I didn't need to resupply, I jumped in. So very unlike me, but I was glad I did. Joking in the gas station mini mart with the other hikers about the absurd food choices and listening to their various trail dramas made me feel like I was actually one of them...right up until I was asked about the slackpack.

We were back at the hostel, sitting around the table enjoying our microwaved Stouffer specials when "Calamity" asked how long it took me.

"Well, by the time I got on the trail, I think it was already 9:00 am. And what time did we leave for the store? Last shuttle leaves at 5:00 pm, right? So that's what?"

My math skills have never been the best, but it doesn't take a genius to realize that it is eight fucking hours. To do a nine mile hike. Without a backpack. I was looking at the sign on the fridge, with its bold letters: "Expect Moosilauke hike to take 5-8 hours" so I laughed and pointed, "Looks like I took the maximum time."

Calamity was sweet, assuring me it's a difficult section. He wasn't the one to make me feel like a loser; it was my own fault I let it get in my head. I felt a fraud, trying to hang with the big dogs. How could I ever think I'd actually be like any of them?

At some point, I snapped myself out of it. At the Hikers Welcome, I had been welcomed. There I was, sitting around a table with all manner of people - breaking bread, sharing wine - how could I let my stupid pride rob me of this experience? I lifted my loaf of Wonder Bread like Jesus at the Last Supper, "Who wants another slice?" It turned out to be a triumphant night after all. My best one yet.

I was supposed to be ready by 8:00 am for my ride back to the trail. It may have only been two nights, but it definitely felt like the last day of summer camp, with its typical running around to collect all the things scattered everywhere. Did I remember my charger? And don't forget the sandals under the bed. Oh yeah, my bread! There was still a half loaf left, and I was so excited to be able to make actual sandwiches with the tuna and mayo packs I had also picked up at the store. It was right here on the table last night...

I found it as I was cleaning up my breakfast plate before leaving. All the deliciously soft, pre-cut slices of chemical goodness were scattered in the compost pile out back. Drop Bear strikes again.

It was another late start, and another fairly steep climb to start the day. With only four days until my meet up with Ken and Leigh, I really had to stay on schedule. That meant 12 miles...12 miles I was really not feeling up to. At a midday break, I noticed something in my guide book notes I had not paid much attention to - the fact that the campsites in the White Mountains actually charge you money. Money I no longer had. The upcoming shelter at only six miles in was my last free of charge option, and after that, I had just enough cash to cover the next two nights.

So after only one day of being caught up, I abandoned the master plan once again. I'm sure the campsites don't turn you away if you don't have cash; they must have a way to bill you later. But you know the truth is it took very little to convince me to stop early. The new plan of 11 miles the following day was no big deal. Yes, I had heard all the warnings of not trying to do over 10 miles in the Whites, and the two upcoming mountains did look pretty daunting, but how bad could it be?

That night a thru-hiker I met at the hostel showed up just before dark. "Legs" was appropriately named, unfairly cruising along on what looked like stilts. He had left the hostel that morning about the time I did, which meant he had completed the mountain it took me eight hours to do the previous day, as well as the six miles I struggled with this day. Annoying for sure, but it gave me a glimmer of hope that the "keep it under 10" rule was overstated.

Foolish Kellbell, forgetting she can not hang with the big dogs. Little did I know how much The Whites were about to punish me for it.

BONA FIDE EMPTY

Have you ever had a moment when you felt you just couldn't keep going? No, I'm not talking about the serious desire to want to end your life, though I've had that as well. If that shocks you, you should consider what Anne Lammont wrote in her last book. In it, she described having the urge to throw herself off every time she was near a high drop off, and when she finally confessed this strange impulse to a friend, their reply was simply, "Who doesn't?" I think feeling overwhelmed with living comes quite naturally to many of us.

But I'm not speaking about that kind of despair. I'm talking about the horrible "I can't do this" exhaustion, except that you know you have to. Maybe it was childbirth. Finishing a term paper? We've all had it. I had it several times on this trip already. But experiencing it at 8:00 am was a new low.

After climbing up the endless rocks on Kinsman Mountain's south side for two hours, I couldn't perceive how I was going to survive the rest of the day. Back to my original slug pace of less than a mile an hour, it would be another 10 hours of hiking, at least. You would have thought my earlier moose sighting would have filled my adrenaline tank, but even that couldn't energize me.

He crossed my path just before I started the steep incline. Seeing something coming towards me ahead on the trail, I assumed it was hikers and stepped aside to let them pass, as I usually do. Nevermind the etiquette that states uphill travelers have the right of way, I was always ready for an excuse to rest for a minute or two. I got out my water, fidgeted with a few straps, waited patiently, but nobody passed by. What could be taking them so long? I stepped back onto the trail to see what was up, and there he was in all his glory.

Due to their mating season, September is the worst month for moose aggression, so I probably should have been more nervous. Instead, I felt only awe. What a majestic creature. He was kind enough to go off into the woods and allow me the right of way, thank goodness.

Mile by mile I just kept moving, though the rest of the day provided all the things that make for an exceptionally hard time. After accidentally getting off-trail yet again, then slipping and hurting my shoulder, I finally came to a sign that said "Liberty Spring Campsites--2.6 miles."

“I got this! I actually got this!” I thought to myself...and then the Stairmaster level went from level five to ten. By the time I was on my last .09 of a mile, I had nothing left. Usually “nothing” means “almost nothing,” as many past experiences have taught me. (Or "mostly dead," if you are a Princess Bride fan.) After reaching the “I absolutely can’t keep going” stage on a few of my previous trips in Washington, I would discover a reserve I didn’t know was in me. I might even declare that phenomenon the most inspiring part of hiking - finding that elusive unknown strength. Only this time, I was not finding it. I tried the counting technique; it only made me realize how hopeless it was to think I could take another 2,700 steps. Before I knew it, I was sobbing. Head down on my poles, just standing there, crying my eyes out. Then the angels showed up.

They circled me, giving me all the comfort their sweet golden bodies could generate. Is there anything on this earth that can bestow the pure love of heaven more than a couple of retrievers?

When their master caught up, I felt embarrassed. Who likes getting caught in such a state of weakness? But she was so kind and encouraging, and even said she had seen a stealth spot just a few yards down where I could set up my tent if I needed. The thought of stopping so close to my goal actually fueled me. I had to keep going. So I dried my eyes, thanked her, and told her I'd see her at camp.

"I'll see you at camp then," she answered in a way that gave me hope it was actually true.

Not 15 minutes later, I was crying again. This time it was legitimate...there really is nothing left. Bonafide empty. No more reserve of strength waiting to be found. How was I supposed to keep moving?

With the help of more angels, that's how.

This time, two gals coming the opposite direction were suddenly comforting me. "You poor thing! Oh, this mile is a killer for sure. You are so close, you can do it! Here, you need to drink this. This water has electrolytes in it. It really helps. You are going to make it, don't you worry."

I realized I recognized one of them from the Upper Goose Cabin. She laughed and said yes, she was Tarzan's girlfriend. She gabbed on about why they were only day hiking as I drank the magic elixir - details I couldn't grasp then and certainly don't remember now. The only thing I could think about was how I knew she was specifically the person at Upper Goose who had gotten so angry that someone had rinsed their plate with all their mush still on it. While she was so kindly trying to nurse me back from the dead, I could only stare at her blankly, absorbed with the idea of giving her my pancake wasting confession. Instead, I gave her a tearful thank you and tried to believe she would still love me even if she knew the truth. The trail had provided once again, therefore I had to conclude my sins had been forgiven.

So four angels and 75 minutes later, I, at last, approached the host at Liberty Springs to give him my money. I had reached punch drunk stage by then...ridiculously giggly and chatty.

You've been there, right? Somewhere in the back of your mind you are asking yourself, "What the hell are you even saying? For God's sake, just shut up!" but your extreme depletion has made you literally high. I talked that poor kid's ear off until he walked me all the way to where I could finally put up my tent.

There was a lot I was curious about though. This whole camp host thing seemed so odd; does he live here all summer? It's not like we were at an RV park or something - this was the side of a mountain. In fact, it was so steep and sloping, the sites were all wooden platforms. Well, except for mine. My tent was very difficult to put up on a platform, so I asked for the one spot that didn't require one, not knowing I'd have to walk what seemed like another mile to get there. Patiently answering my questions as he walked and I hobbled behind him, he explained the deal. He stays a couple of weeks at a time, hikes off the mountain for a few days, then back again - the perfect gig for a student who is an outdoor nut. As we passed the "kitchen" area (a flat-ish spot covered with a giant tarp with two large bear lockers smack in the middle) he made it clear everyone was expected to use it.

It was dark enough to actually get out a headlamp by the time he broke free from my jabbering self, and typically I would have just crawled in my tent and choked down a granola bar with how tired I was. But I determined I'd go back up to the kitchen and make a proper dinner with the group that I knew was already gathered there. The phenomenon of unknown strength never ceases to amaze.

I had my golden retriever friends cozying up and begging for a hand out as I clumsily went about attempting to cook. Lighting your saving angels on fire would have been a sin beyond redemption, so I was extra careful to focus my last remaining brain cells on the task. Dog mom scolded and tried to keep them at bay, but I told her it was fine. It was more than fine.

"Glad to see you made it," she said with a gracious, knowing smile.

MAKING IT TO THE WELCOMING COMMITTEE

Only one more night alone. It was the best thought to wake up to on day 45. The next thought was not so great though: "What if the Garfield Ridge Campsites are full when I get there?"

Social hour in the Liberty Spring kitchen had provided much discussion about the popularity of my next seven miles. The word was that the Franconia Ridge is arguably the best hiking in New Hampshire, and considering it was a Saturday, there would be stiff competition for any spot in the area - especially Garfield. It was mostly locals speaking up; including a sweet woman named Alaina. She was enjoying the great outdoors alone for a few days, and let me know she was also headed to Garfield.

"I've been out here for six weeks, and sure as hell should be able to beat any weekend warriors!" I silently assured myself - though my previous night's performance of a blazing 75 minute mile gave little support for my pep talk. But instead of fretting, I tried to heed my lessons about not imagining the worst. The trail had my back. It would all work out.

The ridge lived up to all the hype. At last, views I could no longer scoff at. Despite the promised hordes that went with it, I couldn't possibly be grumpy. For the first time since New York, I took out sunglasses and basked in the unimpeded sun, allowing my prescription lenses to show me never ending ranges in every direction. It was so overwhelmingly beautiful that I totally forgot I was supposed to be in a hurry.

Not until my last mile, when I saw a group whom I could only assume were also headed to Garfield, did I start to panic. Suddenly I was convinced they would inevitably take the last available spot. The race was on.

Their pack leader was on to me as soon as I passed them. He left his troupe in the dust and was in hot pursuit to beat me. Any Zen notions of believing the trail would provide were flicked away as if a buzzing distraction. I flew down off the ridge with as much focus as a mogul skier.

"Twisting your ankle the day before you meet Ken and Leigh would be a really brilliant move, dumb ass"...but my inner critic was just more head noise to ignore. Nothing could stop me as I planted each pole and catapulted myself from rock to rock.

Convincingly in the lead, I passed the water supply as I made the turn off to the campsites. Having to come back to get water would be the price for victory, which was nearly mine. But then, my nemesis; those last several tenths of a mile that are always straight uphill. NOOOO!!!

I gave it everything I had, but it wasn't enough. He passed me, just when the host's site came into view. I tried to be a humorous good sport while I panted up behind him...making some terrible joke about sharing his tent if he indeed got the last spot. Nothing is worse than trying to pull off funny when you are actually pissed and bitter. It was a devastating fail, in every way.

"I have just the spot for you," the host cheerfully informed me once it was my turn, in spite of my woefully veiled attempts to act as if I wasn't one click away from turning into a screaming meemie. "Another solo female. I'm sure she'll be happy to share her platform," she concluded while pointing to #9 on the map.

And there was Alaina, waiting and greeting me like an old friend. All at once I remembered she had told me she'd save me a spot at Garfield. I suppose I didn't take her seriously. Oh, ye of little faith. Dang, the trail sure has a way of humbling you. Not only did I have a place to legally pitch my tent - being next to Alaina meant my last night alone was already behind me.

For every ounce of excitement built up for day 46, there was a pound of dread for the 14 miles required to reach my welcoming committee. I know, I know...what was I thinking planning 14 miles in the Whites? But this was the only section where I knew it would be doable. Just one difficult up and over, then an unheard-of five miles of complete flatness until Ethan Allan Pond. Still, 14 miles is 14 miles, and there was no question it was going to be a long day regardless.

The one distraction I had going for me was visiting the huts. I had researched each one online, back when I was arranging and rearranging the "master plan" of how I was going to conquer these 50 days. The grand finale of the White Mountains was the crux, the climax, the make or break for everything; and the difficulty in finding a reservation was the reason why the last five days HAD to be what they were. Every hut, except the one we'd be staying at come day 47, had been either full or closing for the season. So getting to see in person each hut that had let me down was like getting a last look at a lover who had scorned you.

Though with the long day ahead, I knew I couldn't linger for long. A quick look around, and an appeal for a handout was all I was after. My internet readings had revealed the huts allow thru-hikers to dine like stray dogs on any of the meal leftovers, and you know despite the death of my overly frugal soul, I was totally into it.

Regrettably, besides one bowl of vegetable soup at the Lonesome Lake Hut on the previous day, all the scornful lovers remained stingy. It was just as well; Leigh promised a meal would be waiting for me at the campsite once I got there. A dinner shared with loved ones...it was too much to think about. But you know I did anyway. Every 30 seconds or so.

Was I going to cry when I saw them? Every time I would watch the "loved ones" episode of Survivor (when the players are reunited with family or friends) I would wonder the same thing...how would I respond if it were me? It's expected you should cry. Crying shows your love. Not breaking down is equivalent to being cold-hearted. Thinking about that pressure always made me glad I wasn't in their situation.

Now here I was, in the "you had better have some tears!" shoes, and it was making me feel anxious. It was hard to predict what my emotions would look like. After some of my long exhausting days, my mental state had ranged anywhere from indifference to behaving like a drunk; so who knows how I'd act. The last thing I wanted was to come off as detached and disappoint the two people who had worked so hard to come and support me.

At the last mile before Ethan Pond, I tried to prepare myself for how long I knew it was going to feel, although knowing I didn't have to worry about any incline must have implanted a small expectation that it wouldn't be so bad. What I didn't expect was to get stuck in a weird time vortex, like in the movie Groundhog Day. It felt like I was going over the exact same long stretches of wooden planks the AT uses for wet sections of trail, over and over again. I've never experienced anything quite like it and actually had to sit down and assure myself the mile MUST come to an end at some point. After all the horrific last miles I'd endured, this one was quite possibly the worst.

"If I don't see the sign for the turnoff in five minutes, I am for sure in an alternate universe...and if these people ahead of me don't move out of my way, I might just run them over," I thought as I plowed ahead like the emotionally out of control person I was. Then I heard them laugh.

"Come on, girl!"

Ken and Leigh, not at the campsite like I had imagined, but hiking towards me. They were here, they were actually right here! Right in front of my very eyes!

"This has been the longest fucking mile of my life," I blurted out before I could check myself. Oh no...here comes the hiking lunatic's disappointing reunion reaction letdown.

But the tears blessedly came; they came in genuine grateful sobs. It was one of the top 10 happiest moments of my entire life.

They had already set up camp, and instead of sitting around waiting, they decided to find and surprise me. The whirlwind of talk as we walked back was like a symphony; words surrounding me with a beauty I'd forgotten the sound of. The comfort you feel when talking to people you feel secure with is something you can't fully appreciate until you are denied it. After not having it for weeks, I felt the full weight of how exhausting it is to be constantly socially tense. Getting a meal prepared for me was as amazing as I had hoped for, but feasting on their stories that were so freely and enthusiastically given was even better. I felt weightless. Having an effortless conversation with people who knew and loved me was like floating downriver - not a care in the world.

Okay, one care. An alarm set for 5:15 am, with 10 miles of the White Mountains to overcome, and not one of them even remotely flat. But now I had my real "tramily" with me. For the first time, I could go to sleep with the thought, "We will finish them together."

AVOIDING THE PLAGUE OF DEATH

If you ask my husband about his experience on the AT, the first thing he will tell you about is the "stifling forest." The first two miles of steep incline we hit in the thick air was a cruel welcome to the discomfort the East Coast has to offer.

We were blessed with a beautifully hot, although typically humid, September day. Hurricane Florence had been on the prowl for days, causing chaos in the Carolina's, and threatening to send all kinds of wind and rain to regions unknown. The White Mountains are notorious for crazy climate changes, so it seemed any disturbance in weather patterns should certainly wreak havoc for us. There are all kinds of signs on the trail to "Turn back at the first sign of bad weather" because of this reputation. I knew I could be robbed of my 500 mile goal if things turned too sour, even while I was on the home stretch. But for now, it was so far so good.

Except for having to deal with the stifling forest. The green tunnel had zero air movement this day, and the steady uphill in the stagnant air left my companions dripping and sluggish. For the first time ever, I lead the pack, and even had to wait for them. It was glorious. I thought I was long past being competitive with my husband - ever since the day I was so happy to at last beat him at ping pong, only to have him confess he was playing left handed. But now I was in the lead, and after feeling like such a loser with the thru-hikers for so long, how could it not feel good to finally prove I had actually gained some speed.

It didn't last long. As soon as we cleared the timberline, Ken was in his element. As a former hardcore rock climber, granite is like home for him. Thank God he only had to endure a few miles of that stifling forest, because 90% of the AT is exactly that. Any other five day portion of the trail would have been his hell. Seeing him light up once we were above it all, atop the rocks and looking down from above like the chief of the mountain goats, made any doubts about the master plan dissolve. It even made losing my fleeting moment of superiority a small price to pay. I had chosen our grand finale wisely.

At one point in the day, we passed a southbounder who looked like she had lost a wrestling match with a bobcat. Trying not to stare at her various scratches and bruises when she stopped to chat for a minute, I finally couldn't help asking, "What happened to you?"

"Maine happened," she said with a laugh. I had read about the difficulties of Maine when I thought that was where I'd be ending. Just a few miles after you leave New Hampshire you'll run into what many hikers claim is "the hardest mile on the AT." The issues I had already faced with rocky portions paled in comparison to the descriptions of the "Mahoosuc Notch," a veritable maze of boulders you need to literally squeeze yourself through in places - like a Mastiff through a dachshund's dog door.

After seeing this poor scraped up soul, I reiterated to myself that I had chosen wisely indeed, and should be very grateful I'd be getting off the AT while I was still ahead...that is if we didn't get pushed off by weather before then. Obviously, things could be a lot worse, and I needed to withhold from complaining about how difficult the rocks were from here on out. If only I had a dime for every time I promised myself I was going to stop whining.

We arrived at Mizpah Spring Hut just in time to get ready

for dinner. By "getting ready" I mean nothing more than changing into our least stinky clothes, as none of the huts have showers of any kind...or flushing toilets, electricity, or private rooms. But they do have excellent food served family-style, which was an indisputable feast.

The huge farmhouse tables seat 12 each, so we had plenty of opportunities for interaction. On this day, the hut was nearly at capacity - filled with mostly school kids on some kind of summer field trip. The handful of us old folks were huddled together in the far corner, trying to make the most of it. As much as I wanted to be chatty and get to know my table mates, I did little more than ask to pass the potatoes. No more free-floating conversation for me. Socially exhausted once again.

The hut hosts interrupted dinner to first announce that the weather forecast was good enough for safe travels. This was not a special briefing because of Florence, it was a nightly routine. Many have perished on the Presidential Range, not because it's particularly high or difficult, but more possibly because it isn't. People head up with shorts and a tee shirt thinking it's no big deal, then get caught in a surprise storm and find themselves in big trouble. Winds at the top have been recorded up to 231 miles an hour - the world record for speed that is not associated with a tornado or tropical cyclone. So getting the clear to hike the next day was certainly a big relief.

After the weather forecast, the hosts introduced the AMC volunteer sitting at our table. He would be giving a talk later in the library on grouse for anyone interested. We looked around at the room full of squirming nine year olds, and Ken whispered in my ear, "Fat chance that's happening."

Later I imagined the sweet man, sitting there waiting to inform anyone willing to listen about the joys of wild game birds, and I wished with all my heart I was kind enough to go, just so he wouldn't be alone. But I didn't even dare peak in the library to see if our suspicions were true. Clearly, my inner asshole was still with me. Though in my defense, none of us had the energy for that level of graciousness. We hit our bunks minutes after dessert hit our bellies.

We were woken to smells of the huge breakfast that awaited us, so getting an early start was out of the question. We lingered, not quite ready for our next dose of mountain punishment, and stayed to ask Bill a few last questions.

Of all of us at the grown-up table, Bill was the only thru-hiker. Probably in his upper 60's, he looked to have left half his weight on the trail. If I could have named him Scarecrow I would have, but he was having none of those fancy trail names. His mother called him Bill, and that's all he needed, thank you very much. He said he'd be pushing on to Madison Spring Hut that day - a far too lofty goal for us. We planned on hiking off the ridge and down below the tree line to stealth camp at a spot I had read about, and could only pray was actually there. With the closure of Lake of the Clouds Hut just the day prior, and without the ability or desire to do the 11 miles to Madison (which I already knew was full anyway) we had no other option. But obviously, Bill knew what he was doing, so we wished him luck and left him behind. We didn't expect to ever see him again, but the Whites would have other plans.

We had two presidents to vanquish; first Eisenhower, then the granddaddy of the entire East Coast, Mt. Washington. We could see it towering above us as we took our lunch break amidst the swarming hive of activity at Lake of the Clouds. Although in the process of cleaning everything out due to having just closed for the season, we were allowed to go in and get water; which we did as quickly as possible because the place smelled like a sewage plant. If you are wondering what is done with all the human waste that goes down those non-flushing toilets, wonder no longer. It's all barreled up and flown out to be reused as compost somewhere. Today was packaging day, and it was one hell of a dirty job. We were sure to cook our lunch a good distance from the fumes.

If only we would have known that the cafeteria we'd find at the top was selling two for one pizza and hot dogs.

I understood Mt. Washington was a tourist destination. After having read a thru hiker's blog, where she complained of having to wait in line to get a picture at the Mount Washington sign, it was obvious the summit was accessible by more than just leg power. What hiker wouldn't be annoyed at having to wait behind the masses who had only walked from the parking lot? My guidebook also had notes telling about the world's first mountain climbing cog railway that could also take you to the top. But somehow everyone failed to comment on the most important detail about the summit of Mount Washington - FOOD, and lots of it.

The Sherman Adams Visitor Center was quite a place. Besides the food we loaded up on, there was plenty to be distracted with. The plaque of death prominently displayed on the wall caught our attention, and we found it difficult to break away from wanting to read about each of the 161 lives that had been lost on the mountain. We pulled ourselves free to make a last stop at the gift store, where Ken couldn't resist a shirt displaying a boastful "Mount Washington/ 6288 Feet." He found it quite amusing, considering that it is barely higher in elevation than his own childhood home in the mountains of California. But enough dilly-dallying; a glance out the observation window at the gathering clouds let us know we had better get going.

It rained just enough to make scrambling down the piles of rock to our stealth site a slippery nightmare, decisively ending my one day hiatus from whining. Not until Ken unpacked his leftover pizza to share with us did I recover from that horrible .07 of a mile, that you know felt more like three.

Getting to Madison Spring on our next to last day was supposed to be the easiest of all our days together. How could I forget that having a mindset of "easy" was a surefire recipe for disappointment? By the time the hut came into view, we were all praying for a miracle of three available bunks, but it was not to be. Knowing we had to detour again to another campsite off trail meant we really needed to hurry so we could secure a spot, but getting out of the cold with a cup of hot soup was too great a temptation, so we all clamored inside Madison and took a seat.

And there, sitting across from us and looking like death, was Bill. What a story he had to tell.

Bill had stayed longer than he should have at Mizpah, then also got lured into loitering at Mount Washington. The night caught up with him, in the worst place possible - the vast talus field you have to maneuver over before finally descending to Madison. We had enough difficulty finding our way across the endless rocks in the daylight, even with the huge cairns leading the way.

At times as big as six feet high and ten feet wide, cairns are the saving sentinels of the trail. These are the "essential to survival" piles of rock that nobody should be knocking down. Looming like ghosts in the misty air, they are always spaced just far enough apart so as to be barely seen through the fog; otherwise, you couldn't possibly know which way to go. Please don't think I'm exaggerating; even Ken, who is very skilled at reading a rocky trail, said this was the first time he knew he'd get lost if not for the gift of the cairns.

With a headlamp Bill might have made it, but it had slipped off his head and down between the rocks after he had taken a fall. There was nothing he could do except hunker down on a boulder, wrap his tent around him, and wait for morning light. Madison made room for him as soon as he arrived, although a day late and now without a reservation; and they were also allowing him to stay another night to continue to recover. He was lucky to be alive, being older and so very thin in the exposed upper altitudes all night. Had he made his mistake a day later, on the much colder and wet night we were about to have, I'm thinking he would have become yet another name on the dreadful plague of death.

Before saying goodbye to Bill to make our own climb down once again, we were warned of how popular, not to mention small, the Valley Way Campground was. Knowing we were in danger of not getting a spot, I felt the repeat panic of my Garfield experience as a couple passed us right at the turnoff. When they dumped their packs at the only seemingly available space to go search for a possible better one, it was all I could do to keep myself from chucking them into the trees. Too bad so sad; saving spots is now officially unallowed.

We did end up getting the spot, but not through sabotage. They left it to us willingly, after apparently finding something superior. How or where, I don't know, because I didn't move. If they would have come back to claim it, after all, they would have had to pitch their tent over my dead body. Figuratively, of course...but barely.

We were fortunate enough to be safe in our tents, crammed onto our tiny 15 x 18 site, before the rain started in earnest. Forty-nine days down; only one more to go. Though I was exhausted and spent on every level, that amazing thought made it all feel worth it.

I'M 50, AND I CAN

We had our breakfast by the fire - the one and only I had made on the entire trip. Ken had created an impressive fire pit in an appropriate looking spot next to our site when we heard that fires were actually allowed. Not until packed up and leaving did we notice the sign showing where the two designated fire rings were. Oops. Thankfully we avoided finding out what the fine is in New Hampshire for illegal fires, as I doubt pleading ignorance would have helped much had we gotten caught.

There were no breakfast scraps left for us stray dogs once we made it back up to Madison, but we sat down anyway to enjoy some hot tea. "Turtle" and "Cat Woman" were there too, a couple we had just passed as they were breaking down their stealth spot half way back up on the Valley Way Trail...and who managed to still beat us there anyway.

Trail couples are the cutest. There's nothing better than adventure love. We couldn't leave without bestowing upon them every ounce of extra food we had overpacked (mostly Leigh's - that girl does not chance not having enough snacks) along with all the well wishes we could muster. Though the 20 or more packs of handwarmers Ken had brought were rejected, (when I texted him before he left to "bring the handwarmers," I didn't mean the entire carton!) so they all went straight into the hiker box. I like to think Bill was still in bed and grabbed them all before he left...just to be on the safe side.

Once we were off the mountain and back in the green tunnel, Ken was not having fun anymore. None of us were actually; me especially. I couldn't help feeling really annoyed that I had to work so hard to keep pace with them. I could accept it when we were on the rocks, those have never been my forte; but downhill in the woods? Fifty days on this bloody trail, and I could still barely keep up? Seriously?

We passed the turnoff to the Osgood tent sites, and then the trail took a decidedly more downward momentum. After quite some time, Leigh asked a question that made me stop dead in my tracks.

"What do the blue blazes mean again?"

"It means we have to go back up this damn hill," I answered. How did I not notice we were on a blue blazed trail? Because Ken was leading, so I had stopped paying attention. Due to all of my horrible mistakes during this hike, I had become fastidious about checking and double-checking at trail crossings; but now I was back to my "acquiesce everything to Ken" default mode.

Once we made it back up to the Osgood cutoff, Ken was sure to point out how misleading the sign there was. Dare I say he was even a little defensive about it? Oh, how I wish we didn't do this to ourselves. We all make mistakes; it's so unnecessary we should pretend we don't, or get upset when we do. In fact, it's in our failures, our weaknesses, our struggles and pain that we find our commonality.

Life doesn't have to be a competition; especially if we really believe that everything we are is simply a gift. The experience of living should be seen through the lens of grace. When it is, we lift each other up, we help, we use our strengths...not to prove our own worth, but for each other. No need to judge or look down upon, because that would be the same as judging and looking down at ourselves. Love doesn't do that.

I wish I could say all that insight fell on me and seeped into my soul, making everything carefree from then on. The truth is, at that moment, I was only relieved to have not been the one who messed up, for once. Sigh...oh, how difficult the ego makes it to love well. Though understanding that this love and oneness is not something I generate, but instead is the truth of God I need only to believe and live out, helps. And how can I not forgive, myself as well as everyone, for how very hard this truth is to actually believe, and to actually live out?

On the last mile, I asked Ken and Leigh to go ahead without me. I wanted to be by myself so I could reflect on the fact that my 500 miles were coming to a close. How could I get my head around it? Part of me wanted to discount it altogether. You know the voice by now, "Wow, 500 miles when a real hiker would actually do the whole thing. Big whoop, hotshot."

Thankfully, I didn't listen. It was okay to be proud of myself. Not a boastful kind of proud; I hope I've already shown there can be a difference. Life offers the opportunity to achieve goals, and embracing that gift with a spirit of gratitude is good and right. Working hard to fulfill a dream feels amazing. Yes, achieving the end result you hoped for is great, but that's beside the point. Forgive me for saying it, but the joy truly is in the journey. The sad part is when the adventure comes to an end.

Except that an ending means a celebration! After my tearful ruminations on what this opportunity had given me, and wrapping up all my loving and hateful thoughts about the wonderfully awful trail that is the AT, I caught up to Ken and Leigh to tell them I had an idea for my last YouTube video. Sending them ahead without me to the Joe Dodge Lodge parking lot, I gave Ken my phone and told him to start filming when he saw me coming out from the trees.

"I just did 500 miles in 50 days when I turned 50...and I can kick...stretch...and kick!" The group of kids who were there as part of yet another school trip looked at me like I was crazy, doing my full kicking and stretching routine; but I knew my friends would appreciate the Sally O'Malley impression, even without the cameltoe. (If you need to Google the SNL skit, you should. It's hilarious.)

Now to let the victory celebration commence! Time for those lodge cocktails I had dreamt about so long ago. Anything with the name Joe Dodge has got to at least have a beer, right?

Wrong. But let me tell you a few things about Mr. Dodge before explaining. I know you are picturing a hick (or maybe that was just me) but Joe got a lodge named after him for good reason. Basically, he was behind all the huts being built or rebuilt, and why they work together cohesively. Oh, and don't forget the weather observatory on top of Mount Washington; that was him too. Plus, I guess he also was known for saving countless hikers on rescue missions. So yeah, he was the man. The Joe Dodge Lodge commemorates this hero the way it should, in the style and fashion of all the huts. A bit more grand, yes - but the food is still served family style, like the rest of the huts. So that meant no actual restaurant...which meant no bar...which meant no cocktails. No celebratory libations for us.

Remember being young and trying to talk adults into going and buying you some alcohol so you could party? How strange it felt to be giving a gal we just met, (who was younger than three of our kids) a handful of money to drive the nine miles into Jackson to buy us booze. Strange, possibly even shady...but worth it. Sitting in front of the library fire, and lifting a strong stout with a toast to an eight year dream that had finally come to fruition - well, it was exactly the finish I was hoping for.

Along with ending 50 days of no sex - a record I hope never to break. Enough said there.

We awoke in the morning to a torrential downpour. The word on the street was that wind speeds would be up to 80 mph on the ridge. Talk about dodging a bullet. The joy may be in the journey, but getting directed off the mountain a day shy of 50 would have been one pisser of an outcome.

As I was standing in line to board the plane home, I suddenly realized I didn't know where I put my boarding pass. Frantically looking in every pocket as I slowly approached the flight attendant, my critical voice chimed in once again, "Wow, you really are still that girl who needs looking after, aren't you?" But it's okay; the thought didn't make me recoil like it once did. Not so much because I now know I can look after myself, but more because I am increasingly able to believe I am indeed always looked after.

My small self (or what I've called the ego, or what some call the false self) will always be whispering in my ear the sweet nothings of judgement, fear, and worry - but I don't have to listen. My true self (what I will simply call "my life that is now hidden with Christ in God") can be trusted to complete the work that has already begun.

In the meantime, I'll keep trying to trust fully that I am fully loved...even the directionally challenged, forgetful, unorganized, and unsure parts of me.

And bigger trust has a way of opening you up to faith in bigger dreams...I did just finish a book about a 76 year old woman who completed the nearly insurmountable Triple Crown, (Grandma Gatewood would be proud) so who knows what adventures lie ahead.

Made in the USA
Monee, IL
25 January 2020

20875096R00106